SEMINAR STUDIES IN HISTORY

Editor: Patrick Richardson

JOSEPH II AND ENLIGHTENED DESPOTISM

SEMINAR STUDIES IN HISTORY

Editor: Patrick Richardson

A full list of titles in this
series will be found on the
back cover of this book

SEMINAR STUDIES IN HISTORY

JOSEPH II AND ENLIGHTENED DESPOTISM

T. C. W. Blanning, M.A., Ph.D

Fellow of Sidney Sussex
College, Cambridge

HARPER & ROW, PUBLISHERS
NEW YORK, EVANSTON, SAN FRANCISCO,
LONDON

Library of Congress Catalog Card Number 76–153472

Printed in Malta by St Paul's Press Ltd for Harper & Row, Publishers, Inc.

Contents

Note on the System of References

A bold number in round brackets (**5**) in the text refers the reader to the corresponding entry in the Bibliography section at the end of the book.

A bold number in square brackets, preceded by 'doc' [**docs 6, 8**] refers the reader to the corresponding items in the section of Documents, which follows the main text.

Acknowledgements

We are indebted to the following for permission to reproduce copyright material:

Birken Verlag for extracts from *Quellenbuch zur Osterreichischen Geschichte* by Otto Frass; Herold Neue Verlag for an extract from *Leopold II, Vol. 1* by Adam Wandruska and extracts from *Der Josephinismus, Vol. 2, Ent Faltung und Krise des Josephinismus 1770–90* by Ferdinand Maass; Franz Steiner Verlag for an extract from *Heiliges Romisches Reich 1776–1806, Teil II* by Karl von Aretin.

Part One

BACKGROUND

Part One

BACKGROUND

1 The Enlightenment and Enlightened Despotism

'Everything must be examined, everything must be shaken up, without exception and without circumspection.' This unequivocal demand, made by Diderot in the *Encyclopédie*, was reiterated by thinkers of the Enlightenment all over Europe. Radical criticism of existing values and institutions was the most prominent and universal characteristic of the Enlightenment. The antiquity of an idea, a law, a privilege or a form of government was no longer regarded as a reliable indication of its excellence. Joseph von Sonnenfels (1737–1817), the most celebrated of the Austrian cameralists, propounded as axiomatic the principle: 'Every tradition which has no justifiable basis should be abolished automatically.' Arguments that the exemption of the nobility from taxation or the clergy from secular jurisdiction were hallowed by time-honoured practice were rejected as irrelevant. Prescriptive right succumbed to the test of utility. Dismissing the efficacy of capital punishment, Cesare Beccaria wrote: 'If it be objected that almost all nations in all ages have punished certain crimes with death, I answer, that the force of these examples vanishes, when opposed to truth, against which prescription is urged in vain. The history of mankind is an immense sea of errors, in which a few obscure truths may here and there be found.' Criticism of the *status quo* was not of course an invention of the eighteenth century; nor did the thinkers of the Enlightenment reject or even question everything they inherited. Nevertheless, the passion and comprehensive scope of their attack entitles one to speak of a qualitative change.

The origins of their iconoclasm were various, but of primary importance was the scientific revolution (**28**). By the middle of the seventeenth century it was clear that the attacks of men such as Copernicus (1473–1543), Tycho Brahe (1546–1601) and Galileo (1564–1642) had discredited medieval science. The synthesis of Newton marked its final defeat. The disintegration of a system which had endured almost unchanged for centuries sent tremors through the whole intellectual establishment. As it was seen that the ancient

3

explanations of the universe and the physical world were demonstrably wrong, although they bore the official stamp of approval of the Roman Catholic Church, intellectuals working in other fields turned from biblical, aristotelean or ptolemaic exegesis to questioning inherited and hitherto undisputed assumptions. Part cause and part effect of the scientific revolution had been the evolution of systematic doubt as a method. It received its classic formulation from Descartes (1596–1650); in the *Discourse on Method* he wrote: 'The first rule [I made] was to accept as true nothing that I did not know to be evidently so.' The deductive and non-experimentalist approach which Descartes adopted and his belief in innate ideas were rejected later by the Enlightenment. Nevertheless, his insistence that truth should be sought and could be attained by the use of man's reason proved to be revolutionary. The philosophes of the following century acknowledged their debt and in Diderot and D'Alembert's *Encyclopédie* Turgot wrote, 'Newton described the lands which Descartes discovered' (**70**). Indeed it was perhaps inevitable that once one part of the establishment cosmology had been dismantled later and more radical demolition teams would extend their operations to all sectors of human life. For all the innovations it witnessed, the seventeenth century was an age of transition; it was not until the eighteenth that men cast away all their inhibitions and used their reason in a wholly autonomous way, without any conscious reference to established religious doctrine (**25**).

Allied to, although not essentially related to, this systematic doubt was the growing popularity of empiricism as a method. Empiricists establish general principles inductively from observation of the facts, rather than apply to the facts general principles which have been arrived at deductively. Popularised in England by Francis Bacon (1561–1626), who was acclaimed by Voltaire as 'the father of experimental philosophy', empiricism made slower headway on the continent, where the all-embracing systems of philosophers such as Descartes and Leibniz (1646–1716) predominated. The startling results achieved by Newton proved to be a persuasive advertisement for the efficacy of the empirical method he propagated. Newton summarised his position thus: 'The best and safest method of philosophising seems to be, first, to inquire diligently into the properties of things and to establish those properties by experiments, and to proceed later to hypotheses for the explanation of things themselves' (**6**). This empiricism was adopted by most of the Enlightenment thinkers and was extended by them from the natural sciences to all forms of human behaviour. They rejected passionately the *a priori* systems of previous centuries; one of the most pejorative adjectives in their vocabulary was 'metaphysical'. Voltaire likened metaphysics to a minuet, in which the dancer displays much grace and elegance but ends up exactly where he started, while the Earl of Shaftesbury asserted that 'the most ingenious way of becoming foolish is through a system'. This adoption of the empirical method contributed to the secularisation of political thought. The criteria for judging political activity were sought not in any supernatural order but in the observable facts of political life. A political philosophy could be constructed without reference to divine revelation.

The development of the critical spirit of the Enlightenment did not occur in an intellectual vacuum. If the targets had not been so ripe for attack the weapons provided by the methodology of the natural sciences would not have been grasped with such alacrity. It was the apparent superstition, inhumanity and irrationality of the *status quo* which sharpened the philosophes' critical faculties, which gave the emotional impetus to their attack. Although Voltaire had eulogised the cultural achievements of the reign of the Sun King in his *Age of Louis XIV*, the reign had also provided ample evidence of the need for political reform. Although Louis XIV and his ministers asserted the primacy of the interests of the state over the individual will of the monarch they failed to translate this principle into practice. The philosophes admired Louis's assertion of the Gallican rights of the French Church against the papacy but much of his activity excited only their disgust. In particular the revocation of the Edict of Nantes (1685) and the forcible conversion or expulsion of the Huguenots were condemned as examples of irrational fanaticism. The appalling suffering made necessary by Louis XIV's ruthless pursuit of personal glory and dynastic ambitions led to a mounting barrage of criticism. The situation in France did not improve after his death in 1715; in many ways it deteriorated. Robbed of its commanding figure at the centre, the *ancien régime* and its anomalies appeared progressively less acceptable to its growing body of critics (**42**).

When analysing the confusion and inefficiency of the state in which they lived, the philosophes were confronted immediately with the problem of privilege. In almost every country in Europe privilege was a peculiarly ubiquitous phenomenon (**53**). Individuals and classes, trading companies and guilds, clergymen and officials, cities and provinces all enjoyed special rights which set them apart from the whole. Defenders of the old order claimed that privileges were necessary for the efficient functioning of society and that they carried with them certain obligations. The noble landowner was exempt from taxation and enjoyed absolute control of his serfs but was obliged to serve his king in time of war and to feed his serfs in time of scarcity. The guild-master enjoyed a monopoly but was obliged to maintain strict control over both his profits and the quality of the commodities he produced. This picture of the corporate society as an interwoven pattern of mutual obligation was attractive but, by the eighteenth century at least, quite misleading. The exploitative element of privilege was developed fully, the reciprocal element largely forgotten. Sanctioned only by customary law and the passage of time, the privileges led to administrative chaos and placed a disproportionate burden on those unfortunate enough to be mere subjects. As many of them were born into the latter category, the philosophes were in an admirable position to appreciate the effects of the *ancien régime's* anomalies. Voltaire's opinion of the privileged classes was not enhanced by a thrashing he received from the Chevalier de Rohan's lackeys after he had made an insulting if witty remark about their master. Apart from individual clashes of this kind, the philosophes believed, with some justification, that the vested interests of the privileged classes formed an insurmountable barrier to the reforms which were needed so desperately.

Radical reform was not advocated in a utopian vacuum. The injustice of the system was apparent to the most casual observer. Repeatedly, the philosophes, as *hommes engagés*, were moved to reach for their pens by some grotesque act of inhumanity on the part of the establishment. In 1761, for example, a young Huguenot of Toulouse called Calas was found hanged in his father's shop. The circumstances and the young man's record of mental instability strongly suggested suicide but the rumour spread that he had been murdered by his father to prevent his conversion to Roman Catholicism. After a perfunctory trial the father was condemned to death, tortured, broken on the wheel and finally strangled by the executioner. This judicial murder became a *cause célèbre*, Voltaire mobilised the troops of the Enlightenment and a vigorous pamphlet war ensued. As a result the elder Calas was rehabilitated in 1765, albeit posthumously. This and other similar cases prompted Voltaire to make a comprehensive investigation into and indictment of the French judicial system (**26**).

Of all the privileged bodies which attracted the hostile attention of the enlightened thinkers the most powerful, the most wealthy and the most thoroughly detested was the Church (**39**). Individual critics had raised their voices in protest in the seventeenth century, but it was in the next century that anticlericalism became an identifiable movement. Although most of the great seventeenth-century scientists had been devout Christians, the methods they employed and the results they achieved were not sympathetic to a religion which relied heavily on divine revelation, on the direct intervention of God in the natural laws of the universe. Opposition by the Catholic hierarchy to the new discoveries, dramatised by Galileo's forced submission in 1633 to the orthodox cosmology in which he could not believe, prompted embarrassing speculation about the validity of all Catholic dogma. Textual criticism of the Bible by men such as Richard Simon did nothing to support the Christian claim that it was the direct word of God, rather than a confused, inaccurate and frequently absurd historical chronicle. Those who rejected revelation but could not bring themselves to adopt atheism found refuge in natural religion or deism. God was demoted from an omnipotent, all-seeing and ever-present being to a distant prime mover of the universe, which now operated according to its own laws. The traditional answer of Catholic scholasticism or Protestant orthodoxy failed to satisfy the increasing number of enquirers. The intricate arguments of the scholastic theologian-philosophers were derided by David Hume as 'spurious erudition' and Voltaire dubbed scholasticism 'the bastard daughter of Aristotle's philosophy'. Yet the protagonists of the intellectual establishment enjoyed a virtual monopoly of control in the universities, the schools, the academies and, above all, the censorship commissions. Seeking to assert the autonomy of reason, to subject everything to criticism, the men of the Enlightenment found their way barred at every step by the entrenched forces of orthodoxy. Any deviation from the straight and narrow path was punished by the confiscation of the offending work and the fining, imprisonment or even exile of its author. In France alone there were seventy-six official censors in 1741. Similar conditions prevailed elsewhere and all over Europe intellectuals who were not Catholic scholastics concluded that the breaking of the Church's stranglehold on means of expression was a pre-condition of enlightenment.

Background

It was not just a feeling of intellectual claustrophobia which prompted attacks on the Church; the specific objects and the emotional fervour of the anticlerical movement were provided by the actual abuses with which the Church was permeated. The reforming vigour of the Counter Reformation had disappeared long since, and the upper echelons had relapsed into complacent opulence, if indeed they had ever emerged from it. Although the vices of the Renaissance popes were not repeated in quite the same spectacular form, there was enough evidence of clerical immorality to gladden the heart of any right-thinking anticlerical. The gross discrepancy between the claims of the Church and its actual performance was as striking in the eighteenth century as ever before. Although the anticlericals seized on the shortcomings of individual prelates as useful propaganda, they were concerned primarily with abuses of more general significance. In particular they attacked the contrast between the prelates, who lived in a manner indistinguishable from that of a secular prince, and the parish priests who lived in a manner indistinguishable from that of a peasant. They argued that the prodigality of the prelates also had a harmful effect on the community as a whole. The collection of tithes to support their extravagance impoverished the peasantry, while the exemption of all the clergy from taxation placed an inordinate burden on the rest of society. The enormous amount of property owned by the Church had a serious effect on the income of the state and the general prosperity of the country. Land once held in the icy grip of 'the dead hands' never returned into circulation. That the interests of the Church were not identical with those of its flock was shown by its claim to be exempt from secular jurisdiction, to be a state-within-a-state. For the anticlerical these abuses were to be found in their most acute form in the monasteries, against which some of their most vituperative rhetoric was directed [**doc. 5**]. Voltaire summarised the monks' contribution to the community thus: 'They sing, they drink, they digest.' Not only did the clergy fail to make a useful contribution to society, they also caused it positive harm. They sought to bolster their overprivileged position by encouraging superstition among the common people. The Enlightenment believed that while the vast majority of the population continued to believe in such absurdities as miracle-working relics and were denied access to the products of rational thought progress was impossible. By their intolerant attitude towards dissent, the priests fostered religious persecution and, quite apart from its inhumanity, a policy of compulsory orthodoxy led to the emigration or expulsion of some of the state's most skilful and industrious members, to the corresponding benefit of its enemies [**doc. 1**]. The charges levelled at the Church were often exaggerated but they had enough foundation to allow the anticlericals to find concrete examples and a receptive audience.

Criticism of the *status quo* was encouraged further by increased knowledge of extra-European cultures. Exploration, colonisation and travellers' reports on China, South-East Asia, Africa or the Americas made Western Europe seem increasingly peripheral and its civilisation increasingly parochial. The discovery that China, for example, had developed a highly sophisticated civilisation before Greece or Rome at least weakened the hitherto confident belief in the absolute superiority and validity of Europe's Christian culture. The philosophes seized on the non-European civilisations with alacrity, for they served both as models and as propaganda. Partly as a ploy to escape censorship, they wrote what purported to be factual travel books, in which they themselves, thinly disguised as Persian noblemen or Red Indian savages, subjected contemporary society to a comprehensive indictment. Voltaire's *L'Ingénu* (1767), Montesquieu's *Persian Letters* (1721), and Diderot's *Supplement to the Voyage of Bougainville* (written 1772, published 1796) were only the most celebrated of a host of such works. In Letter 29 of the *Persian Letters* Rica, a Persian aristocrat travelling through France, wrote to a friend in Smyrna, describing the religious situation in Europe. After a suitably cutting description of the Pope and his powers, he described—with wide-eyed perplexity—the arrogant intolerance of the myriad of churches, all of whom claimed to be the sole depository of truth. He concluded: 'I can assure you that there never was a kingdom where there were so many civil wars, as in that of Christ,' and exclaimed: 'Happy is the land which is inhabited by the children of the Prophet!'

It is easier to describe what the men of the Enlightenment were against, than what they were for; nevertheless, making allowances for the inevitable exceptions, it is possible to arrive at some lowest common denominator. Having abandoned prescription, customary law and divine right, they were faced with the fundamental problem of the origins of legitimate political authority. Most sought the answer in the social contract, given its classic formulation by John Locke in his *Second Treatise on Government*. Few believed that the

9

contract had occurred as an historical event but it served as a useful basis for the construction of a rational theory of political obligation. Joseph von Sonnenfels, for example, argued that to escape from the anarchy which prevailed in the state of nature men formed a civil society based on mutual consent. To provide its members with security against internal and external enemies a coercive force was necessary; according to the terms of the contract the individual members were obliged to obey its dictates. There was considerable confusion as to what form this coercive power should adopt. It is clear that the philosophes' fervent belief in civil liberty and the rule of law was not compatible with support for authoritarianism. Yet their failure to be explicit about constitutional limitations on the power of the ruler and their outrageous flirtations with such absolutists as Frederick and Catherine the Great invited accusations at least of indifference. The theorists of Central Europe were less ambivalent. Unlike their French colleagues, they did not have a literate audience large enough to support them as professional authors. They were compelled to supplement their literary incomes by accepting state employment in the universities and the administration. This had the advantage of giving them practical experience of political problems but did not encourage radicalism. As Sonnenfels wrote: 'For forms of government, I say with Pope, let fools contest! Whate'er is best administered is best!' This opinion was shared by his Austrian compatriot Karl Anton von Martini who argued that once the social contract had been made the subjects could protest only by petitions or by flight. The contractual theory of political obligation was not necessarily liberal.

The most explicit constitutional arrangement was that advocated by the physiocrats, a group of French intellectuals which included such luminaries as Turgot (1727–81), Quesnay, Mercier de la Rivière and Dupont de Nemours (1739–1817) (**50**). Fundamental to their system was a belief in an all-embracing and eternally valid natural order, whose supreme law was the right to self-preservation. The practical expression of this right was the right to property, which could be realised only in civil society. The activities of the ruler, on whom all power was bestowed by the familiar contract, ought to be restricted to the maintenance of the natural order within his dominions. He was an administrator rather than a creator. Dupont de Nemours wrote: 'The legislative power cannot be that of creating but that of declaring the laws.' His power was absolute, in that he had no human competitors, but limited, in that he was obliged to follow the dictates of the natural order. This dual nature of political authority was reflected also in the phrase the physiocrats used to describe their system: 'legal despotism'. There was a curious mixture of liberal and authoritarian elements in physiocracy. The 'despotism' of the monarch was counterbalanced by demands for freedom of the press, for an independent judiciary and for the public conduct of all government business. The other most striking feature of the natural order was the principle that the only true source of wealth was the agricultural 'net product'. This led the physiocrats to insist that the only legitimate form of taxation was a single tax on land (the *impôt unique*), irrespective of the social status of its owner. They argued further that all restrictions on economic activity, such as tariffs, internal customs dues, monopolies and privileged guilds, must be abolished. The physiocrats have attracted a degree of attention disproportionate to their influence on contemporary rulers. Superficial similarity between isolated measures of Joseph II or Leopold II and the physiocratic programme does not allow one to trace a causal connection. The hour of the physiocrats seemed to have come when Turgot was made *contrôleur-général* of France in 1774 but he was dismissed less than two years later. The relationship between *despotisme légal* and *despotisme éclairé* was more verbal than substantial.

The physiocrats believed that the best government was that which did least. This was not an opinion shared by most thinkers of the Enlightenment. Indeed the reluctance to impose constitutional limits on the central power was due partly to the great importance attached to the role of the legislator. Voltaire echoed the views of most of the Enlightenment thinkers when he wrote: 'Almost nothing great has ever been done in the world except by the genius and firmness of a single man combating the prejudices of the multitude.' Confidence in the efficacy of legislative action derived from the Enlightenment's view of human psychology. Here again the influence of John Locke was decisive. In *An Essay Concerning Human Understanding* he had written: 'Let us then suppose the mind to be, as we say, white paper, void of all characters, without any ideas; how comes it to be furnished? Whence comes it by that vast store which the busy and boundless fancy of man has painted on it, with an almost endless variety? Whence has it all the materials of reason and knowledge? To this I answer in one word, from experience, in that all our knowledge is founded and from that it ultimately derives itself.' This rejection of innate ideas opened up boundless possibilities for social engineering. If man was simply the product of his environment acting on his sensations, then to change the nature of man one had only to change his environment. If the average man was ignorant, superstitious, intolerant and brutalised, it was the fault of bad institutions and bad laws, which could be reformed.

This was the task assigned to the legislator; to enable him to perform it he was to be given full powers. Intermediary authorities interposed between him and the individual citizen were to be abolished. The original contract established the subordination only of the citizens to the coercive power, not of one group of citizens to another. Privileges granted by the ruler to certain groups could be removed as soon as the situation required, however long they had been enjoyed. Abbot Rautenstrauch, one of Joseph II's ecclesiastical reformers, wrote: 'The ruler can dispose of everything in the state, without exception. . . . Privileges which are disadvantageous to the state are always invalid.' Above all, these abstract principles were designed to be applied to the two bastions of the medieval corporate order: the nobility and the Church. Not only had they usurped powers which belonged properly to the state but they had exploited their privileged position to the detriment of the general good. Almost without exception, the men of the Enlightenment supported attempts by rulers to reduce or abolish the powers of the intermediary authorities.

Despite this and despite their acceptance of absolutism, they were not prepared to concede arbitrary power to the ruler. He might be given absolute power but it was absolute power to do good only. Yet the dismissal of God from politics necessitated the search for a new standard of political morality. The eternal problem of the dual nature of law—law as command and law as universal moral obligation—required a secular solution. Like many of their predecessors, the thinkers of the Enlightenment sought the answer in natural law, but it was not the scholastic natural law current in the Middle Ages. During the seventeenth century men such as Hugo Grotius (1583–1645) and Samuel Pufendorf (1632–94) completed the secularisation of natural law. Whereas St Thomas Aquinas had made reason 'the handmaid' of faith, the natural law advocates of the eighteenth century gave it complete autonomy. They believed that a system of law could be constructed logically from rational axioms, thus making reason rather than custom or faith the arbiter between justice and injustice. Pufendorf and his followers Christian Thomasius (1655–1728) and Christian Wolff (1679–1754) propagated the new natural law in the German-speaking countries with considerable success. At a time when rulers were beginning to insist that their officials received an academic training, the supporters of natural law quickly gained a predominant position in the German universities and thus acquired considerable influence over the actual conduct of political affairs in the individual states. Although a thinker of little originality, Christian Wolff was particularly influential. Even Frederick the Great, whose detestation of German culture was notorious, was a fervent admirer and he accepted with gratitude Wolff's dedication to him of one of his major works (**79**). Wolff argued that natural law was identical with reason and that therefore every action of the state in accordance with reason was lawful. As the absolute sovereignty of the state was also accepted, the most obvious practical implication of this rationalistic natural law was that the state enjoyed enormous power. Yet in theory at least this power was not arbitrary but lawful (**104**).

In this form natural law was little more than an intellectual abstraction but certain practical conclusions could be drawn from it. Protection for the individual citizen against the possibility of arbitrary excesses on the part of the ruling power was to be assured by the rule of law. The laws were to be in conformity with reason, were to be known and were to be administered impartially. The importance of the rule of law was emphasised constantly by the thinkers of the Enlightenment, who often pointed approvingly to England as a model in this respect. Perhaps the most celebrated illustration of their preoccupation was the following conversation between the Dauphin, the father of Louis XVI, and Quesnay, the physiocrat. The Dauphin observed that the task of a king was very difficult. Quesnay disagreed. 'What?' replied the Dauphin, 'and what would you do, if you were king?' 'I should do nothing, Monsieur.' 'And who would govern?' 'The Laws.' In the *Dictionnaire Philosophique* Voltaire imagined a conversation between an European official and a Brahmin. 'But once more,' said the European, 'which state would you choose?' The Brahmin replied, 'That in which one obeys the laws alone.' 'That is an old reply,' said the official. 'That doesn't make it any worse,' said the Brahmin (**26**).

Pronouncements on justice were not confined to vague declarations

13

of principle; quite specific recommendations were made. The most influential of the many who wrote on the subject was Cesare Beccaria (1738–94), whose most important work—*Dei Delitti e delle Pene* (Crimes and Punishments)—was published in 1764 [**doc. 2**]. Even within his own lifetime it was translated into twenty-two languages. Beccaria adopted a strictly utilitarian attitude towards the judicial process: 'By justice I understand nothing more than that bond which is necessary to keep the interest of individuals united; without which men would return to their original state of barbarity. All punishments which exceed the necessity of preserving this bond, are in their nature unjust.' Consequently he was against torture, capital punishment, informing and sins being treated as crimes and in favour of public trials, equality before the law, prevention rather than punishment and simple well-publicised laws. There was to be a complete separation between the regular political administration of the ruler and the judicial system. Thus even if there were no constitutional checks on the power of the ruler, such as a representative assembly, the interests of the individual citizens would be protected by the rationality and the impartiality of the laws.

Yet most of the thinkers of the Enlightenment did not think merely in terms of limiting the power of the ruler. Proceeding from the principle that a law existed independent of the sovereign's ability to command, it was argued that not only were there certain restrictions on his power but that also he had certain obligations to fulfil. In accordance with the terms of the original contract, he had a duty to promote the general welfare of the citizens. Joseph von Sonnenfels wrote: 'The aim of the men who united among themselves was the individual good, the aim of those who have united is the general good: that is the sum total of all individual goods. In civil societies this good, this aim, is security and comfortable living, which together constitute public welfare' (**45**). This good was conceived of as being entirely secular. The men of the Enlightenment were not prepared to forgo material comfort on earth for the sake of some putative paradise after death. Happiness, *bonheur*, *Wohlfahrt* were among the most frequently used words in their vocabulary; the idea of redemption through suffering was quite alien to them (**37**). Thus they argued that the activity of the state should be directed towards the promotion of its citizens' material well-being.

The belief that this was both possible and desirable stemmed from the confidence engendered by the discoveries in the natural sciences.

With one or two exceptions, the men of the Enlightenment did not believe in the *inevitability* of progress, but they did believe that a rational approach to the problems of human existence would bring progress. In particular the cameralists of Germany and Austria concerned themselves with detailed schemes to improve man's lot. Accepting the principle that overall direction must come from the centre, they adopted a severely mechanistic view of the state. In the words of J. H. G. von Justi (1717–71): 'A properly constituted state must be exactly analogous to a machine, in which all the wheels and gears are precisely adjusted to one another; and the ruler must be the foreman, the mainspring, or the soul—if one may use the expression—which sets everything in motion' (**73**). Consequently, great importance was attached to the need for professional, highly trained and utterly obedient officials. For they were to perform a bewildering multiplicity of tasks. Christian Wolff, for example, required his administration to control immigration and emigration, to establish the number of workers in the various industries, trades and professions, to force people to work, to fix their wages and hours of work, to found and administer schools, universities and academies of arts and sciences, to provide medical care, to set up prenatal clinics, hospitals, institutions for unmarried mothers, poor-houses, orphanages, old people's homes, and so on. He had a detailed plan to meet every imaginable contingency. He observed, for example, that students were prone to drink and frequent the company of women; this was to be regretted because it prevented their working satisfactorily on the following day. It was much better for students to walk in gardens, for during their perambulations they exchanged ideas and information. Therefore, Wolff concluded, the university authorities should lay out attractive avenues (**51**). Cameralism had its ridiculous side but it was also a powerful practical reforming influence (**44**).

The state had a duty to further the material interest of its citizens but it had no right to dictate to them on matters of conscience [**doc. 1**]. Belief in man's right to work out his own salvation and thus in the toleration of heterodoxy was one of the most important articles in the Enlightenment's creed. According to the terms of the original contract, the individual citizens had given up to the central power the minimum number of freedoms necessary for the protection of the state against anarchy; the freedom to choose one's own religion was not amongst them. This fundamental principle was supported by purely utilitarian arguments. Religious persecution was inhumane, unjust, a barbaric relic of the superstitious fanaticism of the Middle Ages; above all it was unnecessary and self-defeating. Heterodoxy was in no way harmful to the state, while persecution served only to swell the ranks of the sect it sought to extirpate. Insistence on religious orthodoxy was positively harmful in that it hindered progress in all fields of intellectual activity. Kant's famous command—*Sapere aude*—could never be obeyed if the state or Church could place restrictions on the exercise of man's reason (**32**). If the dictates of any given religion were true, then no amount of criticism could shake them. Persecution moreover fostered religious controversy, which in turn absorbed in sterile debate intellectual energies which could have been applied more usefully elsewhere. Very often the dissidents were among the most industrious, talented and wealthy members of the state; to expel them was to sacrifice public welfare on the altar of fanaticism. Philip III's expulsion of the Moriscoes from Spain and Louis XIV's revocation of the Edict of Nantes were two favourite examples of the catastrophic effect intolerance could have on the economy. Whether by philosophes, *illuministi* or *Aufklärer*, these arguments were repeated time and time again, in novels, pamphlets, poems and treatises. More than any other cause, toleration was the watchword of the Enlightenment.

Toleration was not intended to lead to an anarchic situation where various intellectual systems competed for predominance on equal terms. The thinkers of the Enlightenment held quite positive views as to what citizens should think and believed that the state had a corresponding right to foster them. Belief in Locke's psychological theory, discussed above, and in the potentialities of man's unfettered reason led to great confidence in the efficacy of education. A properly organised educational system would lead men out of the medieval gloom of prejudice and superstition into the sunny pastures of enlightenment. The state could also be expected to derive from it certain positive benefits. Beccaria, for example, asserted that 'the most certain method of preventing crimes is to perfect the system of education' [**doc. 2**]. The first step towards perfection was the exclusion or at least reduction of clerical influence. In every Catholic country educational institutions, where they existed, were controlled by the Church. The Jesuits, in particular, enjoyed a virtual monopoly of higher education. Their concentration on the classics and on scholastic philosophy and theology was attacked bitterly by the pedagogues of the Enlightenment, with their predilection for secular practical subjects. The clerical teachers were to be replaced by professionals, trained in special teachers' training colleges. Village schoolmasters had been forced to perform menial tasks to supplement their meagre incomes; in future they were to be paid salaries commensurate with their training and responsibilities. The curriculum was to be altered as radically as the structure. The reformers were careful to emphasise the importance of religion but relatively it retreated and the utilitarian ideal of 'the useful citizen' marched into the foreground. Johann Ignaz von Felbiger, one of the most influential educational theorists in Central Europe, wrote that the system must be designed to produce '*a*. honest Christians; *b*. good citizens; that is faithful and obedient subjects of the authorities; and *c*. useful people for the community' [**doc. 3**]. To accomplish this a host of new subjects was to be introduced, including mathematics, natural sciences, accounting, modern languages, geography and business management. In addition special institutes for mining, architecture, agriculture and commerce were advocated. However meagre his natural talents, rational education could enable every man to contribute to the general good.

Any summary of the political ideas of the Enlightenment invites the charge of distortion through omission or overgeneralisation. One of the most important features of Montesquieu's political philosophy, for example, was his insistence on the need for representative intermediary authorities. Nevertheless, the Enlightenment was cosmopolitan in its outlook and universal in its manifestations. There was one regional variation, however, which needs to be emphasised. For reasons which will be discussed in the next chapter, the thinkers of central Europe and Italy enjoyed a closer and more cordial relationship with the secular powers than their colleagues in France. They were concerned less with attacking or imposing restrictions on the establishment than with assigning it and helping it carry out certain positive tasks. This was an important difference but one of emphasis rather than essence. Austrian, French or Italian, the protagonists of the Enlightenment united on a programme of toleration, the rule of law, social welfare, secular education and opposition to privilege. Its implementation was expected to lead to Kant's celebrated definition of Enlightenment: 'man's escape from self-incurred tutelage' (**32**).

The relationship between this intellectual movement and the

legislation of the eighteenth-century rulers known as 'enlightened despots' is as problematic as any assessment of individual motivation and the relationship between thought and action. There was certainly no reign of the philosopher-kings envisaged by Plato in *The Republic*; the 'enlightened despots' were far from being disinterested executors of a preconceived political philosophy. Quite apart from their intrinsic intellectual value, the reforms advocated by the Enlightenment thinkers were *useful* for the rulers (**68**). Larger armies, more sophisticated weapons, more luxurious courts and inflation compelled a search for fresh sources of income. As there was a limit to the amount that could be squeezed from the peasants and urban commoners, the obvious solution was the abolition of noble and clerical exemption from taxation. This required the emasculation of the estates and the subjection of the Church to the control of the state. It was also clearly desirable that the commercial and industrial potential of the country be realised. This required the destruction of the privileged status of the guilds and the granting of religious toleration, in order to attract skilled and wealthy immigrants. The ability of the peasants to pay state taxes could be enhanced considerably if they were given protection against exploitation by their lords. This required the abolition or at least amelioration of serfdom. To implement these reforms a professional bureaucracy was needed. This required a radical reconstruction of the educational system, with the predominance of religion and the classics making way for subjects with a practical application. To enable the new officials to perform their tasks properly, the administrative apparatus at the centre and in the provinces required a thorough overhaul. A further corollary was judicial reform, with particular attention being paid to correcting the confusion between the regular political administration and the patrimonial jurisdiction exercised by individual nobles. It is possible therefore to explain most of the policies commonly regarded as being characteristic of 'enlightened despotism' in terms of *raison d'état* rather than the Enlightenment. It must also be remembered that these policies were not novel. Rulers who had governed decades and even centuries before the Enlightenment became an identifiable movement had attacked the privileges of the nobility, had secularised church lands, had granted religious toleration, had reformed the administration, and so on. Viewed in this way, the 'enlightened' in 'enlightened despotism' appears as a gloss, as a subtle but mendacious piece of public relations on the part of the monarchs and their ministers.

This interpretation is popular but fallacious. Ultimately a discussion of the relationship between thought and action must cross the boundary which divides the writing of history from philosophical speculation. Such an enterprise is beyond the scope of this book and the ability of its author. Some remarks of a rudimentary and specific nature however can and must be made. It is wrong to assume that there was always a natural antagonism between the Enlightenment and the efficiency of the state. The men of the Enlightenment believed that the destruction of the barriers of privilege, ignorance and superstition would lead to the galvanisation of the latent energies of the state. The happiness of the individual citizens and the power of the state were seen to be interdependent. The problem of the state/society dichotomy, which has been a recurring feature of modern political debate, was not a major preoccupation of the Enlightenment. The argument that any given piece of legislation had nothing to do with the Enlightenment because it increased the power of the state reveals a misunderstanding of the Enlightenment in particular and the nature of political philosophy in general. A corollary of this argument is that 'no man is an island unto himself'. The assertion that the intellectual environment within which a man is educated and grows to maturity influences his subsequent political decision is not necessarily deterministic. It is legitimate to conclude that a ruler has been influenced by theoretical treatises if it can be shown that he has read them with approval and that their recommendations are mirrored in his legislation (**79**). It is as naïve to concentrate on considerations of *raison d'état* to the exclusion of the intellectual milieu as it is to concentrate solely on the latter. The exclamation of Goethe's Dr Faust—'Zwei Seelen wohnen, ach! in meiner Brust' ('Two souls, alas! dwell within my breast')—is as applicable to monarchs as it is to scholars. This is not to suggest that in any conflict between practical considerations and intellectual demands the former would not triumph. Usually they did. Nevertheless, the direct influence of the Enlightenment can be detected in the legislation of numerous European rulers in the second half of the eighteenth century. If one accepts Fritz Hartung's definition of enlightened despotism—'a form of government strongly influenced by the philosophy, and particularly by the political philosophy of the Enlightenment'—then this is all that is required to give the concept reality. These necessarily abstract remarks should be made clearer by the following account of the career of Joseph II, who unlike the other enlightened despots refused to admit a necessary conflict between Enlightenment and *raison d'état*.

2 The Inheritance: Maria Theresa and the Origins of Josephism

In 1684 Philipp Wilhelm von Hörnigk, an Austrian official, published a pamphlet entitled *Oesterreich über Alles, wann es nur will* (Austria above everything, if only it wants to be). Its success was both immediate and lasting; in the course of the following century it went through sixteen editions. Much of its success was due to the peculiar tenacity of the problems it discussed and sought to solve. In 1787, as in 1756, as in 1740, as in 1684, the Habsburg emperors never succeeded in mobilising the vast potential resources of their dominions. This failure was all the more striking in the eighteenth century because it had opened in a blaze of justifiable optimism. The victories of Prince Eugene in the War of the Spanish Succession and his successful campaigns against the Turks had gained enormous acquisitions of territory. In 1718 these included Belgium, Croatia, Slavonia, Transylvania, all Hungary, the Duchy of Milan, the Grand Duchy of Tuscany, Naples and Sardinia. This could have served as the basis for the establishment of hegemony in Europe but the decades which followed brought one military humiliation after another. In 1788 the Austrian army proved incapable of defeating even the Turks. This failure is not explicable merely in terms of the rise of other powers, such as Russia and Prussia; primarily it was a failure in internal organisation.

The Thirty Years War and the terms of the Treaty of Westphalia persuaded the Habsburg emperors that the opportunity to destroy the autonomy of the German princes had gone for ever. They turned their attention to the East—to expansion at the expense of the Turks and to the transformation of their amorphous empire into a unified state. The empire idea (*Reichsidee*) gave way to the state idea (*Staatsidee*). The election and coronation of the Elector Charles Albert of Bavaria, a member of the Wittelsbach family, as Holy Roman Emperor in 1742 was the final proof for the Habsburgs, if it were needed, that they would never achieve hegemony in Germany and that they were entirely dependent on their own territories. The decision to create a unified state was easier to take than to execute. Acquired at various times and in varying circumstances, the component parts of the Habsburg Empire were stubbornly proud of their provincial idiosyncrasies and fiercely opposed to any attempt to impose uniformity from above. During the 1670s, the Hungarians, led by Emmerich Thököly, made a separate agreement with the Turks and assisted them in their campaigns against the Austrians. Similar acts of what the latter called treason and the Hungarians called patriotism were committed under the leadership of Rakoczy in the War of the Spanish Succession. Although these insurrections were suppressed, the opportunity to destroy finally provincial privileges was not taken. Nor were particularist loyalties confined to the more recent and peripheral of the Habsburg acquisitions. The Tyrol and Carinthia, for example, were as jealous of their traditional privileges as were Hungary and the Netherlands. In this very important sphere very little progress had been made by 1740.

The task of imposing unity on a collection of fractious provinces would have been formidable enough at any time; in the late seventeenth and early eighteenth centuries it was made more difficult by the social and economic decline of central Europe. Partly this was due to the long-term movement of the axis of the European economy to the Atlantic seaboard. Although the amount of physical destruction caused by the Thirty Years War has often been exaggerated, it did dislocate commerce and industry in Germany and the Habsburg territories and had a catastrophic effect on the availability of capital. The Habsburgs made the situation worse by their persecution of the protestants. More than 40,000 were expelled from Upper Austria alone and approximately 150,000 left Bohemia. As a result of this mass migration the society they left behind them became more aristocratic, Catholic and static than it had been previously. The forces of tradition were strengthened further by the crusading impetus of the *Reconquista* in the Balkans. While in western Europe religious strife made way for *raison d'état* and the scientific discoveries prompted growing criticism of Christian dogma, in the Habsburg territories the spirit of the Counter Reformation was sustained far into the eighteenth century by the war against the infidel. Austrian successes gave fresh meaning to the idea of the Church militant here on earth. It was a period of flamboyant self-confidence, which found its most lasting expression in the magnificent baroque palaces, churches and monasteries of Fischer von Erlach, Lukas Hildebrandt and Jakob Prandtauer (**66**). Nor was this enthusiasm for baroque forms of art and religion confined to wealthy noble patrons. It was a period of redoubled popular enthusiasm for Mariolatry, for the cult of picturesque saints, for pilgrimages, for processions, for every kind of sensuous religious experience. Although this movement, which engulfed all sections of society, left behind it great works of art, the spirit it engendered was not conducive to the mundane tasks of economic expansion and administrative reform. While the more ambitious rulers followed the example of Louis XIV in creating centralised bureaucratic administrations, the Habsburgs and their subjects remained wedded to their cosy baroque *Gemütlichkeit*, lulled into a sense of false security by their victories over the Turks.

In the fifteen years of peace which followed the Peace of Passarowitz of 1718 Charles VI (1711–40) was presented with a golden opportunity to attend to the internal reform of his territories. In the early years of his reign at least Charles showed a keen interest in economic affairs but he did nothing to create an efficient administration (**103**). In part this was due to his preoccupation with the problems of succession. His failure to father any male heirs prompted a frantic attempt to persuade the various estates of his realm and the European powers to accept the Pragmatic Sanction. This document proclaimed the indivisibility of the Habsburg territories and designated his daughter Maria Theresa as his heir. By dint of strenuous diplomacy and numerous concessions, general acceptance was achieved, but, as the events of 1740 were to show, promises in international relations are broken as often as they are made. The consequences of his neglect of domestic affairs were demonstrated by the Austrian performance in the War of the Polish Succession (1733–8) and the war against the Turks of 1737–9. By the treaties of Vienna and Belgrade, Austria lost Naples, Sicily,[1] Lorraine and much of southern Hungary; the acquisition of Parma and Piacenza by way of compensation was small comfort. When he died in 1740 Charles VI left his daughter a badly led, badly trained and badly equipped army, an administration hardly worthy of the name, large debts and only 87,000 gulden in cash, and a collection of paper promises from the great powers that they would not pursue their own advantage. On 5 November 1740 Frederick the Great wrote to his ambassador

[1] Sicily had been exchanged for Sardinia in 1720.

in Vienna: 'The Emperor is dead, the [Holy Roman] Empire like the House of Austria is without a Supreme Head, the finances of Austria are in a state of confusion, the armies decayed, her provinces sucked dry by war, plague, famine and by the terrible burden of taxation they have had to bear up to the present.' Maria Theresa herself wrote later that in 1740 she was 'without money, without credit, without an army, without any experience or knowledge of my own and finally without any kind of advice' (**98**).

Maria Theresa entered into this miserable inheritance without the benefit of a vigorous ministry to support her. She was a political innocent of twenty-four, while her ministers were experienced to the point of senility. Sinzendorf, who had ruled the chancellery for three decades, was seventy; Stahremberg, the head of the treasury for thirty-seven years, was seventy-seven; Landmarschall Harrach was seventy-one, while his brother Joseph, the president of the war council, was a stripling of sixty-three. Whatever their services to their country in the past, they were not the men to provide effective opposition to Frederick the Great. By the summer of 1741 the Prussian armies had overrun Silesia and the seizure was recognised formally by Austria in the Treaty of Dresden of 1745. Despite Maria Theresa's personal courage in the face of almost overwhelming odds, the loss of her richest individual province was nothing less than a disaster. Silesia's population was over a million and the province had paid 25 per cent of all direct taxation collected from the Bohemian and Austrian lands. The humiliating defeats suffered at the hands of the protestant upstart had at least one beneficial result; they convinced even the most traditionalist Austrian official that internal reform was inevitable [**doc. 4**].

In Count Friedrich Haugwitz Maria Theresa found a man who was determined to apply to the Habsburg Empire the techniques which had proved so successful in Prussia. His main objective was financial, to tap more efficiently the immense resources of the various provinces. The main obstacle was the estates, who were understandably reluctant to pay more to the central government than could be avoided. To circumvent their control of taxation, Haugwitz sought to secure long-term grants, to impose strict government control of collection and expenditure, to reapportion the burden of taxation and to break the fiscal immunity of the nobility. A precondition of success was the reform of the central and provincial administrative bodies. The Bohemian and Austrian chancelleries were united in the *Directorium in Publicis et Cameralibus*, which controlled all aspects of domestic policy. Only the administration of justice was reserved for a special authority. The most senior of the new provincial bodies were the 'Representations and Chambers' (*Repräsentationen und Kammern*) but the most important were their subordinates, the 'Circle Authorities' (*Kreisbehörden*). The tasks assigned to the chief officials of the latter, the 'Circle Captains' (*Kreishauptleute*) showed clearly the military motivation of the reorganisation. They were to supervise the billeting of the troops which passed through their areas, control the prices of military commodities and ensure that peasants were not so oppressed by their lords that they were unable to pay their taxes. The military/fiscal objective of this protection afforded to the peasantry was stated quite explicitly.

These reforms, the first period of *Rétablissement*, achieved something; revenue collected from Bohemia, for example, increased by 25 per cent between 1739 and 1763 (**113**). However the success was at best partial. Any pattern imposed retrospectively on the reforms flatters the insight of their creators. Many of Haugwitz's fiscal innovations were dictated by short-term considerations and had to be reversed shortly after their implementation (**99**). Little progress was made towards the curbing of the selfish particularism of the estates. Styria, Carniola, Görz and Gradiszka granted money for only three years, the Tyrol for only one, while Carinthia refused to make any advance grant. Only Bohemia and Moravia, the provinces most directly threatened by Prussia, complied with the government's demand and voted a fixed sum for ten years. The recalcitrant provinces had to be forced into line. The superficial clarity imposed by the administrative reforms concealed a welter of provincial variation. Hungary, the Netherlands, and the Italian possessions had not been affected at all, while in the reorganised provinces many of the old abuses remained. As the most important officials were still recruited mainly from the ranks of the local nobility, the administration continued to be more loyal to the province than to the central government. Compared with the situation in 1740 enormous progress had been made but the Monarchy was still a long way behind Prussia and many western European states.

The relative backwardness of the country was revealed again in the Seven Years War (1756–63). Although possessing an overwhelming advantage in terms of men and material resources, and although supported by the two largest powers on the European continent, Austria proved incapable of reversing the verdict of 1740. This failure could not be blamed solely on the ineptitude of her Russian or French allies or on the military genius of Frederick the Great. The Austrian military and administrative machine had failed again. Perhaps the most eloquent illustration of the need for more and more radical reforms was the rout of 70,000 Austrians by 35,000 Prussians at the battle of Leuthen in 1757. Even before the war was over the second *Rétablissement* had begun. The first step was the creation of a central Council of State (*Staatsrat*) in 1760. Presided over by Chancellor of State Prince Kaunitz and consisting of eight senior officials, the new council had a purely advisory function. It was to investigate all other official bodies, supervise their activities and draw up plans for their reform. It was to be the progenitor of a revitalised Austrian state. Kaunitz wrote to Maria Theresa: 'I am deeply convinced that only this institution can provide Your Majesty with the means of saving the state, of leading the internal regime away from the disorder and decay in which it finds itself and towards a degree of perfection, which prevails in perhaps no other European government.'

The Council of State's first step towards the translation of this expression of intent into practice was the reorganisation of the central authorities. Finance and general administration, which had been combined in the *Directorium in publicis et cameralibus* were separated again. The Directorium itself was abolished and replaced as the most important administrative body by the United Bohemian-Austrian Court Chancellery (*Vereinigte böhmisch-oesterreichische Hofkanzlei*), which combined both legislative and executive functions. Its encyclopedic responsibilities included security, police, censorship, roads, transport, industry, municipal administration, hunting, forestry, postal services, coinage and ecclesiastical affairs. Five other central bodies were created or retained: the foreign office (*Staatskanzlei*), the supreme court, the treasury (*Hofkammer*), the accounting office (*Hofrechnungskammer*) and the council of war. In the provinces the Representations and Chambers were replaced by ten *Gubernia*, which were subdivided into judicial, financial, commercial and fiscal departments. The Circles, the next and by far the most important links in the chain of authority, were left intact. As in the first period of reform, the object of this further reorganisation was the creation of a unitary state, whose component provinces responded simultaneously and uniformly to orders issuing from Vienna. Again some progress was made. The control of the estates over legislation and taxation declined further to the point of extinction, the administrative autonomy of the towns was finally destroyed. In theory at least Maria Theresa and her officials enjoyed a monopoly of political power in the state.

Despite the efforts of Haugwitz, of Kaunitz, of the Council of State and of individual officials in the provinces, Austria failed to attain 'a degree of perfection, which prevails in perhaps no other European government'. This was due to deficiencies in both structure and personnel. Not surprisingly, it soon became clear that the United Bohemian-Austrian Court Chancellery was as cumbersome in performance as it was in name. Over-concentration led not to greater efficiency but to greater delay. Additional bodies were set up to relieve the Chancellery but too often they proved to be ephemeral. A committee to discuss the economy (the *Staatswirtschaftsdeputation*) was set up in 1769, only to perish seven years later in another reshuffle. Failure to discover the optimum distribution of power at the centre was less serious than the failure to create an efficient bureaucracy. In theory the arm of the state could reach out to touch every subject within its boundaries; in practice it was often reduced to palsied twitching. The previous predominance of the estates in local government and the lack of any appropriate educational system had led to an almost total absence of properly trained and experienced officials. Consequently the central government was forced to rely either on incompetents or on nobles whose loyalties were at best divided. Measures against such abuses as bribery and 'understandings and partialities' between imperial and manorial officials had only limited success. Maria Theresa herself lamented: 'It is always the fault of those provincial officials who do not do their duty . . . thus countries go to ruin.'

The situation in Hungary in 1780 showed how incomplete the progress towards a unitary state had been (**97**). By temperament and by conviction the empress was inclined to compromise with the forces which opposed her and she avoided a direct confrontation with the Magyar nobles. She sought instead to neutralise their ethnic loyalties by transforming them into a court nobility. A contemporary observer noted:

The proud Hungarians, who on their country estates were

engaged in planning schemes of liberty, have been allured to court or to town. By the grant of dignities, titles and offers of marriage, and in other ways, every opportunity has been given them of spending their money in splendour, of contracting debts, and of throwing themselves on the mercy of their sovereign when their estates have been sequestrated. . . . Having thus converted the most powerful part of the Hungarian nobility into spendthrifts, debauchees and cowards, the Court has no longer occasion to fear a revolt.

Simultaneously the central authorities in Vienna surreptitiously extended their control over Hungarian affairs. Subtle though this policy of '*douce violence*' might appear, it was largely a failure. As events in both France and Hungary at the end of the 1780s were to show, the confining of nobles to a gilded cage did not necessarily blunt their political ambitions, especially when the *status quo* was threatened. In the absence of the Hungarian Parliament, which Maria Theresa omitted to summon during the last fifteen years of her reign, real power in the country was exercised by the gentry in their county organisations—the *comitati*—not by the magnates. That the Hungarians appeared to be acquiescent during her reign was due to the lack of any demands being made on them. Magyar separatism was resting, not dying.

The clearest indication that the reformers' dream of a unitary state had not been realised was the continuing financial weakness of the Monarchy. Despite the periodic administrative reorganisations income failed to keep pace with expenditure. Hungary continued to enjoy its privileged fiscal position, the rest of the Monarchy continued to bear a disproportionately heavy burden and the treasury continued to suffer. Maria Theresa inherited a large deficit; she passed on a larger one. Partly this was the direct responsibility of the empress. Incorrigibly extravagant, she showered gifts, sinecures and estates on the sycophantic courtiers around her. In 1755 the Prussian Grand Chancellor reported to Frederick the Great: 'the most serious accusation that can be levelled at her is that her heart is too soft: she ought to be rather less generous and open-handed. What comes in from one direction, from the new financial institutions, flows out in the other, through the rewards she heaps on the very men to whom she owes this increase in her income. I have seen enormous sums spent in this way.' Some improvements were made in both the structure and the techniques of the various fiscal departments. At Joseph's insistence, his father's immense personal fortune was devoted to the reduction of the interest on the National Debt to a relatively modest 4 per cent. Compared with the other European countries, however, the Habsburg Monarchy still resembled an oilfield before the invention of drills. The gap between Prussia and Austria had narrowed by 1780 but it was still a chasm.

In all the various stages of the reform it is difficult to detect any great influence of the Enlightenment. Defeat by Prussia provided the original impetus and the military/fiscal object of the whole operation was made quite explicit. The unitary state was aimed at not because of any opposition to privilege on principle but because it offered the only chance of recovering Silesia. Men like Haugwitz and Kaunitz admired the philosophes but no correlation between what they read and their administrative reforms can be established. Certainly their ruler's attitude to the Enlightenment was one of outright hostility. As a dedicated Catholic of the most rigid kind, Maria Theresa shrank from any compromise with the heretics. She wrote: 'I shall not be led by any spirit of persecution but still less by any of indifference or toleration, as long as I live; and I should like to live only until I can go to the vault of my ancestors with the consolation that my son will be just as great, just as religious, as his predecessors.' She had a particular loathing of the Jews. On the occasion of an edict of 1777, which forbade any Jew to settle in Vienna without her written permission, she wrote: 'I know of no worse plague for the state than this nation of deceivers and usurers.' With some justification, Professor Padover has dubbed her 'a fanatical and bigoted reactionary' (**100**).

This verdict on the person of the empress should not be extended to embrace her reign. Whereas Prussia under Frederick the Great was a personal absolutism, in which the views of the king were of paramount if not exclusive importance, the Habsburg Monarchy was a ministerial absolutism (**145**). On account of its size, heterogeneous ethnic composition and lack of a professional administration, a great deal of scope was left to the individual official. Even had Maria Theresa possessed the necessary will-power and ability, she would have found it impossible to impose her will alone on her amorphous collection of territories. Despite her strongly held opinions, or prejudices, she was also susceptible to influence and there grew up around her a group of men attached to the Enlightenment

29

and determined to translate their principles into legislation. The common cause which united these men was Jansenism in its widest sense, that is opposition to the Jesuits, to ultramontanism, to scholasticism and to baroque forms of piety. Even in the seventeenth century individual priests and laymen had advocated reform but their voices were drowned by the chorus of Counter-Reformation militancy. It was not until the 1730s and 1740s that something approaching a movement became discernible. Jansenism spread in a number of ways. Austrian priests exposed to its influence in the universities of northern Italy and the Austrian Netherlands returned to the Hereditary Lands to spread the word. Religious orders attached to the Jansenists' favourite saint—Augustine—also proved receptive. Most important were the Praemonstratensians, whose largest houses were in the Netherlands and many of whose members had studied at Louvain. Their discontent with the Catholic establishment was shared by many Augustinian Hermits and Dominicans (**112**).

If the movement had remained confined to religious affairs and monastic protagonists it would not have merited more than cursory attention. In the course of Maria Theresa's reign, however, its supporters came to occupy positions of real power at the centre and to extend their interests to all spheres of political activity. The key figure was Gerhard van Swieten, born and educated in the Netherlands and a dedicated Jansenist. As a young man he had enjoyed the patronage of Kaunitz, who at the time was minister in Brussels, and in 1745 he was called to Vienna to become Maria Theresa's personal doctor. He quickly became her informal adviser on other topics, using his influence to secure the appointment or promotion of other reformers. Among the most important were Karl Anton Martini, who was made Professor of Natural and Roman Law at Vienna in 1754; Ambrose Stock, who became director of theological studies in Austria; Ignaz Müller, who was appointed extraordinary confessor to the empress in 1767; Anton de Haën, who was brought from Belgium to be Professor of Medicine; Johann von Sperghes, who was a councillor in the Foreign Office and many other lesser officials, priests and journalists. Known collectively as 'the Great Ones' (*Die Grossen*), they showed at an early stage that they had both the will and the ability to take effective action. A good example of this was their seizure of control over the censorship commission, after a protracted struggle with the Jesuits. Appointed to the commission soon after his arrival in Vienna, Van Swieten scored an early success by persuading Maria Theresa to release Montesquieu's *De l'esprit des lois* for publication. The appointment of Stock and Martini brought him powerful allies and by 1764 the last Jesuit had been removed from the commission (**99**).

Van Swieten and his friends were also very much concerned with education. It was apparent to all the reformers that a precondition of Austrian rejuvenation was a trained bureaucracy. It was equally apparent that this did not exist and that if the educational system continued to be dominated by Jesuits, with their emphasis on the classics and abstruse problems of scholastic philosophy and theology, it was never likely to exist. To supply the missing officials a comprehensive reform was drawn up and an unusually determined attempt was made to implement it. The first step was the establishment of a Ministry of Education (*Studienhofkommission*) with the initial task of secularising the universities. Directors of faculties were appointed to revise both the curricula and the teaching staff. In the purge which followed, the Jesuit monopoly of higher education was broken and adherents of the Enlightenment secured the choicest appointments. Van Swieten was personally responsible for the reform of the medical faculty only, but through his influence over Maria Theresa, he directed the reforms in other subjects as well. Of the new appointments at Vienna the most important were those of Martini and Joseph Eybel in law, of Paul Joseph Riegger in canon law and of Joseph von Sonnenfels in applied political science. Changes in personnel were accompanied by changes in the curriculum. As the need for bureaucrats was the motive of the reforms, there was a corresponding emphasis on practical subjects such as modern languages, accountancy, mathematics and political science. In 1770 a separate institute for the training of merchants, *Realhandlungsakademie*, was set up. The enthusiasm for relevance found expression even in the training of priests. Abbot Rautenstrauch, a prominent member of the Van Swieten circle, devised a curriculum for the theological faculty which, as he said, would liberate the students from the sterile scholastic disputes, and 'let them learn only that which is useful for the cure of souls and consequently for the good of the state.' For the same reason it was ordered in 1778 that even non-Catholics be admitted to degrees; the good of the state knew no denominational restrictions.

Lower education was reorganised along similar lines. In the

grammar schools radical plans for the total exclusion of clerical influence foundered on the simple objection that there were not enough lay teachers but the addition of subjects such as history, geography, mathematics and German destroyed the predominance of divinity and Latin. More remarkable was the attention paid to the education of the masses. The plans for the new teachers' training college were drawn up by Johann Ignaz Felbiger, who was brought to Vienna from Silesia in 1774. An educational reformer of European repute, Felbiger was insistent that every citizen must learn to make a useful contribution to the community. In a theoretical treatise published only two years before his arrival in Vienna he emphasised that a good citizen must 'willingly and gladly do everything conducive to the honour and best interests of his ruler, obey the authorities and officials placed over him by the latter, submit to their laws, orders and decisions and carry them out to the best of his ability even if he cannot appreciate how such orders might benefit him and his fellow-citizens' [**doc. 3**]. Despite a determined attempt to put this severe utilitarianism into practice, Felbiger's commissions found the inherited weight of ignorance difficult to dispel. In many places the teachers themselves were only semi-literate, absenteeism was rife, and in the further reaches of the Monarchy life went on untroubled by instructions issuing from the centre. The main opposition to the new system moreover came from the intended beneficiaries—the common people, who suspected that the innovations were ungodly. Clearly it would be several generations before the reformers' ideal of a unanimously enlightened and loyal society would be realised.

The relaxation of censorship and the new educational policies suggested that either Maria Theresa was very easy to manipulate or that she was not so bigoted as has sometimes been supposed. Her attitude towards ecclesiastical affairs suggested that the latter was the case. The empress was undeniably a woman of strong prejudices; she was antisemitic, antiprotestant, anti all kinds of heterodox opinion. She was a woman of deep and conspicuous piety. Yet she shared the views of her Jansenist advisers that the state should extend its control over the Church and that powers usurped by the national hierarchy or the Pope should be repossessed forthwith. As early as 1751 she had written that the Church should be given no more land, because it had too much already, administered what it had badly and because the monasteries accepted too many idlers. These

assorted abuses required 'a major remedy'. Perhaps the best summary of the official view of Church–State relations was contained in
the instructions given to Cardinal Herzan, when he was sent to
Rome as ambassador to the Holy See in 1779:

> The limits of the power of the Church are determined by its
> sacred object; this, like its ultimate aim, is purely spiritual and
> consists in the preaching of Christian teaching on faith and morals,
> the administration of the sacraments, the conducting of church
> services and internal church discipline. All other power, apart
> from these spiritual objects, which is possessed and exercised by
> the Church, its leaders and its supreme head, the Pope, does not
> come from its original divine institution but from the voluntary
> conferment or pious indulgence of the temporal sovereigns, and
> can, in accordance with changes in the times and other circum-
> stances, be restricted, modified or removed again, in so far as the
> common good of the state requires (**7**).

It is of course highly unlikely that Maria Theresa herself composed this piece or that she was the initiator of the ecclesiastical
reforms but at every stage her approval was required and it was
obtained. The real driving force came from the chancellor of state
Prince Kaunitz, who was concerned primarily with foreign policy
but who also took a great interest in ecclesiastical affairs. As a
disciple of the philosophes, rabid anticlerical and probable atheist—
he was often known as *il ministro eretico*—Kaunitz was convinced that
the privileged status of the Church was the cause of all of Austria's
problems. It was his aim to destroy its position as a state-within-a-
state, to subordinate it completely to state control and to divert
much of its vast material resources into the coffers of the treasury.
The Habsburg Duchy of Milan, where opportunities for friction with
the papacy were abundant, was selected as his laboratory. In 1765 a
new body—the Giunta Economale—was set up, staffed by secular
officials, to deal with all matters concerning Church and State. A
series of ordinances aimed at the reduction of church property followed. In 1766 it was decreed that all estates acquired by the Church
since 1716 were to be subject to the same taxes as secular lands and
that if the clerical body concerned was unable to raise the necessary
money then the land in question was to be sold. This was followed in
1767 by a new amortisation law, which forbade the regular or secular

clergy or lay congregations to acquire property in any form whatsoever. Numerous amortisation laws had been issued before but the scope and severity of that of 1767 placed it in a different class altogether. At the same time all monasteries were ordered to send to the Giunta Economale an exact specification of their members, resources and income. As the monks surmised gloomily and correctly, this was the prelude to the dissolution of a number of 'unnecessary' houses [**doc. 5**].

Reaction from the papacy to these and other measures in the same vein was predictably violent. Strong protests were interspersed with pathetic appeals to Maria Theresa's Catholic conscience, but, although she wavered occasionally, Kaunitz, her son Joseph, Van Swieten, Müller and the others were able to keep her on the straight and narrow path of secularism. The surest indication of this was the extension of measures first tried in Milan to the Hereditary Lands. In 1769 a new department was set up in the United Bohemian–Austrian Chancellery, based on the Giunta Economale and called the *Concessus in Publico-Ecclesiasticis*. It turned its attention first to the monasteries. Like all good anticlericals of the eighteenth century Kaunitz reserved for the monasteries a loathing of peculiar intensity. By their celibacy, withdrawal from the world, idleness and exemption from taxation, the monks not only contributed nothing to the community but imposed an enormous burden on the lay members of society forced to provide for their upkeep. These parasitical anomalies, argued Kaunitz, should be treated like any other civil society and in the interests of the whole reduced in size or abolished. Throughout the 1770s a stream of hostile ordinances sought to accomplish this. Among the most important were a severe amortisation law and regulations that novices had to be at least twenty-four years of age before they made their profession of vows, that all theological studies in monastic houses should be conducted in accordance with the enlightened principles of the University of Vienna and that all links between Austrian and foreign monasteries should be severed. The *Concessus in Publico Ecclesiasticis* also betrayed strong Jansenist influence in its attempts to simplify religious life in the Monarchy. The number of religious festivals was reduced, numerous pilgrimages were abolished and various restrictions were placed on the lay brotherhoods, which were held to be the chief perpetrators of flamboyant religious practices. Indeed, what is usually known as 'Josephism' had a lot less to do with Joseph II than is commonly supposed. Its theoretical basis had been fully articulated by Kaunitz by 1767 and many of its implications had been worked out in practice in Milan and the Hereditary Lands in the 1760s and 1770s (**108**). The empress did not play a great constructive role but without her approval or at least acquiescence nothing could have been achieved.

Hanging like a dark cloud over all these attempts at reform was the problem of serfdom. Both then and now the task of definition has proved peculiarly difficult. Most peasants owed some sort of dues to the lord but these dues could vary not only from province to province but from village to village. Generally, in return for a piece of land the serf was obliged to perform certain services for his lord, the most onerous of which were labour services. These *robota* varied from one to three days a week during most of the year but could reach six days a week during harvest. The serf also paid dues for the use of the rivers, forests and meadows and usually was obliged to sell his produce to the lord, to have his corn ground at the lord's mill and to buy his liquor from the lord's cellar. Heirs wishing to inherit their father's property had to pay death duties (*mortuarium*) to the lord. In addition the lord exercised all civil and criminal jurisdiction over his serfs, collected state taxes from them and ordered their conscription. The serf could not marry, leave the estate or change his profession without his lord's consent. In a year of bad harvests these burdens made the serf's position intolerable. In qualification it must be emphasised that serfdom in this most acute form was not as ubiquitous as is sometimes supposed. There was none in Belgium, where contemporary travellers commented on the prosperity of the peasants; there was none in the Tyrol, where the free land-owning peasants proved to be more reactionary than the highest born aristocrat, and in the central core of the Hereditary Lands—Austria, Carinthia, Carniola and Styria—it was sporadic in distribution. It was only in the more peripheral provinces—Bohemia, Austrian Silesia, Galicia, Moravia and Hungary—that serfdom was the norm (**99**).

Maria Theresa's reformers were opposed to serfdom for a number of reasons, the most important being simply fiscal. As the economy of the Habsburg Monarchy was predominantly agricultural, the main burden of taxation was borne by the peasantry. Yet as the serfs were compelled to spend much of their time working for the lord and most of their income in paying the various feudal dues, there was very little left for the state. Protection afforded to the serfs was protection afforded to the treasury. For more indirect reasons mercantilists believed that serfdom formed an insuperable barrier in the way of the industrial expansion of the Monarchy. A society based on serfdom was a static and a stagnant society; static because it precluded social mobility, stagnant because it precluded a rise in the birthrate. Allied to these practical considerations was the feeling that the meanest serf was not an animal to be exploited but a human being to be treated accordingly. The political philosophy of the Enlightenment, with its emphasis on the contractual nature of political obligation, aversion to privilege and emphasis on man's autonomous reason, could only be hostile to an institution whose only justification was its antiquity. Joseph von Sonnenfels wrote:

> Despotism of oppressive princes over people is a horror. Yet the most obnoxious, the most intolerable despotism is the one which citizens exercise over their fellow-citizens. This was serfdom—that stain on the constitution where it is tolerated, that stain on an alleged jurisprudence which reasoned man down to matter and fabricated faked evidence. . . . How by every aspect of reason, could people even for the sake of protection of their life, ever have wanted to sell what is the greatest, the only value of life? (**90**)

Although the need for reform was recognised by Maria Theresa's ministers it was some time before action was taken (**95**). One of the side-effects of the administrative reforms which followed the loss of Silesia was that for the first time the serfs came into direct contact with the central government. The extension of the authority of the local officials over the manorial estates however had a more theoretical than practical significance. In the face of noble intransigence and official incompetence no real progress could be made. Decrees such as that of 1751 which forbade the lords to expropriate serfs' holdings or that of 1770 which ordered the lords to allow the serfs to buy their holdings outright were not worth the paper on which they were printed. On the royal domains, freedom of movement, marriage and profession was granted and many new holdings were created but this only scratched the surface of the problem. The need for real action as opposed to pious gestures became acute in the 1770s when a series of disastrous harvests created a revolutionary situation in Bohemia (**113**). Joseph II acquired firsthand knowledge of the intolerable conditions there during a tour of inspection in 1771 but he found it impossible to goad the cumbersome bureaucratic machine into taking countermeasures. It was felt necessary to consult with the Bohemian estates, who predictably embarked on a successful policy of obstruction. The peasants then took matters into their own hands. Throughout 1774–5 a violent jacquerie raged across Bohemia. Although aware that the peasants' grievances were justified, the government in Vienna was compelled to send an army to suppress the rising. As with most peasant uprisings the gains did not justify the suffering. In the summer of 1775 a Robotpatent to regulate the forced labour dues was issued but it was only partially implemented. Similar patents were promulgated for Silesia in 1771, Lower Austria in 1772 and Styria and Carinthia in 1778. As in Bohemia, it was found to be almost impossible to persuade or compel the lords to comply. Similarly, Maria Theresa's appeals to the lords to grant their peasants security of tenure were ignored. Towards the end of her reign she gave enthusiastic support to a scheme devised by Councillor Franz Anton von Raab. He proposed that personal serfdom should be abolished, the robot commuted and the lords' demesnes divided into small-holdings to be rented to the peasants for cash. The 'Raab System' was introduced on a number of crown estates in Bohemia but the conservative lords declined to follow suit. Nothing at all was done to remedy the other main grievance of the peasants—insecurity of tenure. It had been recognised that there was a problem and that it was the duty of the state to provide a solution; in this limited sense Maria Theresa's reign represented an advance. On the other hand her own equivocation, the entrenched power of the nobility and the weakness of the local administration left most serfs as miserable in 1780 as they had been in 1740 (**84**).

Like the ecclesiastical reforms, the attempts at legal reform betrayed the dual influence of the Enlightenment and *raison d'état*. Conditions prevailing in 1740 were as diverse as the territorial structure of the Monarchy itself. The customary law which had evolved over the centuries reflected the dominance of corporate groups in provincial life. Not only the sovereign but also the Estates, the Church, the towns, the guilds and the individual landowners exercised jurisdiction of some kind. There was no procedural uniformity, no clear demarcation lines, no division between public and civil law and no comprehensible system of appeal. As an essential corollary to their administrative reorganisation, the reformers sought to seize for the state a monopoly of political power, a monopoly of public law. The modern notion of legal sovereignty, of a central agent with the exclusive ability to command and compel obedience, was to replace the old concept of law as the sanctification of customary socio-economic relationships. In the political sphere, law was to be equated with the will of the sovereign, with the essential proviso that it be conformable with reason, with Natural Law. Subjects were to gain some sort of protection against despotic acts on the part of the ruler by the complete separation of public law, which dealt with the relationship between sovereign and subject, from civil law, which dealt with the relationship between individual subjects or groups. Once the laws governing this latter 'private' sphere had been made rational and uniform by a process of codification the sovereign and his agents would be powerless to intervene (**104**).

The first step towards the implementation of this policy was the creation in 1749 of a Supreme Court (*Oberste Justizstelle*), which was completely separate from the highest administrative body—the *Directorium in Publicis et Cameralibus*—and its successor the United Bohemian–Austrian Court Chancellery. The principle of separation was applied also to the provinces, where a clear and independent system of appeal courts was established. The main problem however remained one of codification. The Compilation Commission which was set up to solve it encountered the opposition of every vested interest in the Monarchy. The provinces, the estates, nobles, towns or guilds were understandably reluctant to abandon their judicial privileges for the benefit of the state and their less fortunate fellow-citizens. Typically, Maria Theresa decided on a compromise. The Codex Theresiana, finally published in 1766, was a mixture of rationalist innovations and corporate relics. As a result enthusiasm for the new code was confined to those who had drawn it up. It was attacked not only by conservatives but also by such enlightened reformers as Kaunitz, Martini, Sonnenfels and Riegger. Attempts were made by the latter group to force the revision of the code but no further progress was made during the reign. The uneasy compromise between tradition and the Enlightenment was also apparent in the Criminal Code issued in 1768. Although it introduced order into a chaotic situation, it retained barbaric penalties for what enlightened opinion refused to regard as serious offences, such as blasphemy, witchcraft and heresy. One real advance was 'the abolition of torture after concerted pressure from a group led by von Sonnenfels.

During Maria Theresa's long reign the Habsburg Monarchy had taken its first reluctant and hesitant steps towards a modern central-ised state. While the social structure and location of power remained unchanged, all kinds of reforms were at least initiated. If their full implications had been developed, the Habsburg Monarchy would have been transformed from a loose collection of provinces, whose social ethos was corporate, clerical and conservative, into a unitary state, whose social ethos was individualistic, secular and progressive. The relationship between the legislation and the Enlightenment was less nebulous than many historians have asserted. There can be little doubt that the original impulse was supplied by the loss of Silesia or that the reforms owed a great deal to common sense, Austrian tradi-tions, the example of Frederick the Great or the exigencies of the situation. Yet the dismissal of the influence of the Enlightenment as coincidence or gloss is explicable only in terms of gratuitous cyni-cism or overconcentration on the personal role of Maria Theresa. Within the loose structure of power at the centre it was possible for adherents of the Enlightenment such as Kaunitz or Van Swieten to put their principles into action. Their colleagues Martini, Sonnen-fels, Riegger or Eybel did not confine their energies to teaching or the writing of theoretical treatises but gained real influence on the conduct of affairs through their membership of the various com-missions (**112**). However limited, the educational, legal and eccles-iastical reforms all testified to their success. Kant's judgment of Prussia under Frederick the Great is applicable to Austria under Maria Theresa: 'It was not an enlightened age but it was an age of enlightenment.'

The attitude of the empress towards the reforms conducted in her reign was as equivocal as their success. She was obsessed with the desire to be avenged on Frederick the Great; for this reason she supported the modernisation of her state. On the other hand, when she met with opposition from the privileged orders she was always inclined to compromise. Combined with the feebleness of the bureaucracy and the strength of the vested interests, this lack of resolution left most of the problems of the reign unsolved. Joseph II, who became emperor and co-regent on the death of his father Fran-cis I in 1765, believed that his mother's worst enemy was her own timidity and that the opposition would succumb to a vigorous exercise of will-power. He was never allowed to test his theory during her reign, for although he was technically co-regent, Maria Theresa always retained the power of ultimate decision. As a result the relationship between the two rulers was curiously volatile, oscillating from an extreme of mawkish sentimentality to an extreme of violent hostility (**100, 3**). Together with Kaunitz and the other enlightened ministers, Joseph succeeded in influencing his mother but as the best years of his life slipped away and the reform movement made little discernible progress he became increasingly impatient. His prospective subjects looked forward to Maria Theresa's death with fear or joy, for they were under no illusions as to Joseph's intentions. As one observer, Baron Risbeck, wrote: 'As soon as Joseph stands alone at the helm, a revolution will take place here, that will render the present inhabitants a phenomenon to the next generation' (**11**).

Part Two

JOSEPH II AS SOLE RULER: 1780–90

3 The Unitary State

Joseph was thirty-nine years old when his mother died in 1780. His chafing at years of political impotence, allied to a natural uncongeniality, had made him economical in the use of what little charm he possessed. It was possible to admire Joseph; it was not possible to like him. For contemporaries his most objectionable characteristic was his sublime confidence in the infallibility of his own judgment. His brother, Leopold of Tuscany, provided the following merciless description of this aspect of Joseph's character: 'He tolerates no contradiction and is imbued with arbitrary, brutal principles and the most severe, brutal and violent despotism. . . . He despises everything which is not his own idea and likes and wants around him only those men who have no talent, who obey like nothing more than mere machines and who give him the credit for everything that is done.' During two extended visits to Vienna in 1778–9 and 1784 Leopold composed two long pieces on the state of the nation and the state of the emperor. They were written in code, which was a wise precaution on Leopold's part, for his brother was depicted as being arrogant, vain, capricious, intolerant, cruel, bad-tempered, conceited and selfish (**110**). Almost certainly, this judgment was soured by a fraternal inferiority complex, but it was confirmed by other and more objective observers. One mitigating circumstance was Joseph's desperately unhappy personal life. His adored first wife, Isabel of Parma, died after only three years of marriage. He wrote to his brother Leopold:

'I have lost everything. The wife I worshipped, the object of all my love, is no more! You know how much I loved her and will be as upset by this tragedy as I am: You can guess what sort of state I am in! Distressed and depressed to an extreme, I hardly know whether I am still alive. What a terrible separation: shall I survive her? Yes, of course I shall, but only to be unhappy for the rest of my life.'

Two years later, in 1765, the demands of diplomacy forced the embittered Joseph to contract a second marriage with Josepha of Bavaria, a woman of breathtaking ugliness. However grotesque she may have been, Joseph's comment, when urged to sire an heir: 'I would try to have children, if I could put the tip of my finger on the tiniest part of her body that is not covered with boils', was unforgivable. After her unlamented death in 1767 he confined his sexual activities to a brief, daily and utilitarian encounter with his gardener's daughter. Without children and detesting his numerous brothers and sisters, Joseph was a harsh and lonely man long before he reached middle age. His bitterness was accentuated by persistent bouts of ill-health, which grew worse in the 1780s and which were rumoured to have their origins in a venereal infection. The energies he might have devoted to his family were diverted instead to his work. He approached the conduct of business with the same devotion to duty that characterised all his other pursuits, often working eighteen hours a day. His passion for work left him no time and less inclination for the pageantry of court ceremonial. In 1787, for example, it was forbidden to kneel before the emperor or to kiss his hand, on the grounds that these servile practices were not compatible with the dignity of man. At the other end of the scale, Joseph showed a remarkable desire and ability to associate with his humbler subjects. He discussed politics with them in the streets and threw open the imperial gardens to the general public. This aversion to etiquette, privilege and snobbery, which was Joseph's most appealing characteristic, was reflected in both his political philosophy and practical policies.

'At birth we inherit nothing from our parents but animal life. Thus king, count, burgher or peasant, there is not the slightest difference.' This assertion of human equality was fundamental to all Joseph's political theorising. When men sought to escape from the anarchic state of nature by means of the social contract, the only kind of subordination they recognised was that of subject to ruler. Subsequent variations in social conditions or political structure could be explained by history but could be justified only by the test of utility. Failure to appreciate this simple fact was due to centuries of accumulated ignorance, which in turn was attributable to the control by the vested interests of the means of communication and education. Joseph believed that the clear light of reason could eliminate from consideration all useless conventions and, having wiped the slate clean, could construct in theory and in practice a perfect state. For him any kind of prescriptive right was anathema. In the atomised society there was no room for separate groups, for they were selfish by definition. Every subject from the meanest serf to the highest aristocrat, had to forgo his own individual interest and work for the common good, the original aim of the social contract. After a tour of inspection in Bohemia, Joseph wrote that it was his aim 'to unite all parts of the Monarchy in a joint enterprise, namely the contributing towards its common good.' Given the selfishness of man, this supreme object could be achieved only by vesting all power in one agency at the centre. The ruler was to be both executive and legislature, enjoying a veritable monopoly of public authority. To enforce his enlightened commands and to ensure that no one shirked his duty, an army of officials was to cover the country. In the interests of the whole their powers over the individual approached omnipotence. The state based on corporate groups (*Ständestaat*) was to be replaced by a unitary state (*Einheitsstaat*). To objections that his ideal was nothing more than an overgrown workhouse, Joseph would have replied that a high end requires high means. For him, bureaucracy, duty and public welfare were interdependent concepts. The enormous power exercised by the sovereign and delegated to his officials was restricted by their duty to promote the welfare of the subjects.

Joseph was not given to abstract speculation; this brief summary is drawn from his correspondence and the preambles of his ordinances. The originality of his views is not striking. In one form or another, all can be found in the works of such contemporary writers as Martini, Sonnenfels and Riegger. The novelty of Joseph's ideals lies only in the uncompromising manner in which they were expressed and in his ability at least to attempt to put them into practice. Their origin is more problematic. There can be no doubt that he was influenced strongly by the Austrian Enlightenment. Surrounded and educated by men such as Van Swieten and Martini, it was inevitable that Joseph should accept much of their teaching. As was argued in the previous chapter, 'Josephism' was expounded fully by the time Joseph himself reached intellectual maturity. Also influential were Muratori's two great works—*Della regolata devozione dei cristiani* (1747) and *Della pubblica felicitá, oggetto de' bouni Principi* (1749). To complete a cosmopolitan spectrum worthy of the Enlightenment, Joseph read, admired and even visited the French philosophes. Although these intellectual influences were of great importance, to portray him as a philosopher-king of the Platonic variety would be palpably absurd. However great his contempt for the past, he was neither thinking nor working in a vacuum. There were long Habsburg traditions, for example, of reducing the privileges of the nobility, of curbing provincial autonomy and of extending the power of the State over the Church. The example of other monarchs, whose relationship with the Enlightenment was non-existent, was also important. In theory at least, Louis XIV had asserted the supremacy of the interests of the whole over those of the ruler and had anticipated Frederick the Great and Joseph's self-appointment as first servants of the state (**69**). Finally, and most important of all, Joseph was consumed by a lust for power which owed nothing to the pacific political philosophy of Voltaire or Sonnenfels. A militarist of formidable dimensions, his enthusiasm for military affairs and desire to cut a figure on the field of battle bordered on obsession. He appreciated also that the power of his state could be increased only by a comprehensive and radical internal reorganisation. To assess the relative importance of these various considerations is impossible. Yet to concentrate solely on the purely practical and historical explanations of his reforms is to distort the history of his reign. As the following analysis of his reign will show, to minimise the influence of the Enlightenment is to commit the paradoxical error of pushing cynicism to the point of naïvety.

Joseph's first priority was the creation of an efficient bureaucratic machine but, after the reforms undertaken during his mother's reign, there was little more to be accomplished in the Hereditary Lands. Finance and administration, which had been combined in 1749 and divided in 1762, were united again. As a result the United Bohemian–Austrian Court Chancellery controlled all affairs of state except foreign policy, the military and justice. The organisation of provinces was rationalised further so that now the Monarchy was divided into thirteen administrative units: Galicia and Bukovina, Bohemia, Moravia and Austrian Silesia, Lower Austria, Inner-Austria (Styria, Carinthia and Carniola), Tyrol, Further Austria (the Habsburg possessions in south-west Germany), Transylvania, Hungary and the Banat, Croatia, Lombardy, Görz, Gradisca, Istria and Trieste. The most important innovation in this sphere was the final eradication of the influence of the Estates. All that remained of the once-dominant bodies were two 'representatives' who served in the office of the Gubernia and whose only link with the Estates was pecuniary, in that the Estates paid their salaries. In a formally administrative sense Görz, Gradisca, Austrian Silesia, Moravia, Bohemia, Galicia, Bukovina, Lower and Upper Austria, Tyrol, Vorarlberg, Styria, Carinthia and Carniola formed one state.

Joseph found more scope for his reforming energies in Hungary, which in 1780 bore a closer resemblance to an independent state than to a Habsburg province (**97**) [**doc. 8**]. The Hungarian constitution was distinguished by two characteristics; it was very old and it was very aristocratic. However unjustified, the fervent belief that it dated back to St Stephen fortified local resistance to Habsburg encroachments. More striking was the restriction of all political rights to 'the nation', a singularly inappropriate euphemism for the nobility. At the apex of the constitution stood the Parliament (*Reichstag*), divided into two houses. In the upper house sat the representatives of approximately three hundred magnate families and in the lower the representatives of approximately 25,000 gentry families. The rest of the inhabitants were referred to as the *misera contribuens plebs*. Although the magnates enjoyed enormous incomes, real power in the country was exercised by the gentry. Not only did the former spend most of their time and income in Vienna, but the Hungarian Parliament was not convened after 1765. In the absence of this central legislative body, power reverted to the counties (*comitati*), which were firmly in the hands of the gentry. By their monopoly of the county assemblies (*congregationes*) and thus of local appointments, the gentry enjoyed absolute control over the administration, justice, education and the Church. As one traveller accurately observed: 'The boasted freedom of Hungary is only a privilege of the nobility and the clergy, to live at the expense of the whole country.' In principle, an administration based on local privileged assemblies was the utter negation of the unitary state Joseph aimed at. In practice it also proved to be inefficient and inhumane. In 1782, for example, the county of Hont condemned 115 male and female gypsies to death on suspicion of cannibalism. Numerous barbarities of this kind suggested that Hungary was ripe for reform. Joseph had indicated his dissatisfaction with the *status quo* when he refused to be crowned in 1780. This insult to Hungarian national pride was followed swiftly by another, when in 1784 the Crown of St Stephen was removed from Pressburg to Vienna. The explanation, that its security was endangered by the conversion of its previous resting-place into a

General Seminary, rings hollow even today. These petty assertions of Habsburg centralism were only the prelude to a comprehensive reform of the Hungarian administration, which began in 1785. The country was divided into ten provinces, the division being made solely on the numerical basis of population, not on that of tradition or geography. The *comitati* survived only in name, being rearranged subdivisions of the province. The old officials, previously elected from amongst themselves by the nobility, were replaced by imperial commissars to rule the provinces and by imperial *Vizegespane* to rule the *comitati*. Their powers were all-embracing and their orders were issued from Vienna. The nomenclature may have been different but in effect the administrative system of the Hereditary Lands had been transported *en bloc* to Hungary.

Joseph's passion for uniformity was not confined to structural externals. In 1784 a decree ordered that in all provinces, except Lombardy and Belgium, German was to be the only official language. In the past officials had been free to use the language of their districts. Now even where the German-speaking inhabitants constituted a minority—in Czech Bohemia, Polish Galicia, Italian Görz and Gradisca, and polyglot Hungary—all official transactions were to be conducted in the language of the centre. No racial prejudice lurked behind the measure; it was simply a matter of administrative convenience: 'Everyone can easily appreciate how advantageous it will be for the general welfare if the same official language reigns throughout the Empire; as a result the bonds of fraternal love will unite all parts of the Monarchy, one with another.' As events were to show, exactly the opposite result was achieved.

In Belgium, where not even a minority of Germans resided, it was impossible to propagate 'fraternal love' in this way, but the archaic administration did not escape Joseph's attention. Justly described by R. R. Palmer as 'a museum of late-medieval corporate liberties', Belgium was a rationalist's nightmare (**72**). The traditional privileges of each of the ten provinces were confirmed by the emperor on his accession, the most celebrated of the charters being the *Joyeuse Entrée* of Brabant. The liberal measure of autonomy promised by them was defended tenaciously by the provincial estates, consisting of the nobility, the prelates and the wealthier burghers. The authority exercised by the imperial representatives—the governor, and his more important deputy, the plenipotentiary minister—was severely restricted. Despite the historical and geographical differences which separated Brussels from Vienna, Joseph was determined to reduce Belgium to the same uniform level as that of his other dominions (**100**). In 1787 a series of innovations cut a swathe through the tangled thicket of Belgian particularism. At the head of the new administration stood the General Council, appointed and directed by Vienna. The old provincial divisions were replaced by nine regions, which were administered by intendants and were sub-divided into localities, administered by commissars. The role of the intendant was equivalent to that of the governor in the Hereditary Lands or the commissar in Hungary, while the Belgian commissar was the counterpart of the Austrian *Kreishauptmann* and the Hungarian *Vizegespan*. The estates were reduced to impotence, their main function being confined to the registration and automatic approval of imperial edicts. Finally, Joseph's remorseless steam-roller also destroyed the various privileges of the municipal corporations. As an essential corollary of this administrative centralisation, the judicial functions of the nobility and other favoured groups were abolished. As in the Hereditary Lands, justice was separated from administration and given its own independent and professional organisation. In the narrow sense of organisation, Belgium was now identical to any other part of the Monarchy but, as in the case of Hungary, the sepulchral calm which reigned before Joseph set to work made the ensuing explosion seem correspondingly more violent.

Another recent Habsburg acquisition to benefit or perhaps to suffer from Joseph's passion for uniformity was the Duchy of Milan (**109**). Although not as baffling in its complexity as that of the Belgian provinces, the administrative structure of the Duchy was an affront to any rationalist. In 1740 very little had changed since Charles V published the *Novae Constitutiones*, the corpus of Milanese laws and customs, at the beginning of Spanish rule over the territory. The social and political elite was the patriciate of the city of Milan, whose members controlled the two most important official bodies—the Senate and the Magistrato Camerale. Although in principle the former was restricted to judicial functions and the latter to fiscal matters, there was in practice a great deal of confusion. There was no separation between the regular political administration and the administration of justice. Together with the other central bodies, the Senate and the Magistrato Camerale enjoyed a good deal of autonomy. They were organised on a collegial basis, that is each councillor had the right to vote on any issue, they exercised full powers

49

within their area of competence, and their members were appointed for life. The individual provinces within the Duchy also enjoyed considerable autonomy and, as in Belgium, resisted fiercely any encroachments by the centre. Representatives of all the provinces met in the Congregatio dello Stato, a corporate bastion against centralism. By his control of appointments and the budget, the Habsburg emperor possessed very considerable theoretical power but his representative in the Duchy—the governor—found himself enmeshed in a web of custom. It was not until the reign of Maria Theresa that an attempt was made to reform the administration. The Italian Council in Vienna, a collegial body which had acted as a representative of the Duchy rather than as an instrument of the centre, was replaced by a bureaucratic department of the Chancellery of State. The powers of the Senate and the Magistrato Camerale were circumscribed more strictly and justice was separated from administration. Milanese autonomy had been restricted but not abolished and it was left to Joseph to make the familiar clean sweep. In 1786 he abolished the Novae Constitutiones, the Senate, the Magistrato Camerale, the Congregatio dello Stato and all provincial and municipal privileges. In their place he established the Consiglio di Governo, which was divided into six departments and which controlled all branches of the administration. The Duchy was divided into eight uniform provinces, ruled directly by imperial officials. The old-judicial structure was abolished in its entirety and was replaced by a coherent system with three stages of appeal, together with the criminal code already operating in the Hereditary Lands. This reorganisation was as drastic as that of Belgium and Hungary but it did not provoke the same violent response. The new administrative system was certainly more efficient and the new judicial system was certainly more just but they reinforced the impression that Milan was ruled by a foreign power. Even some of the senior officials thought that Joseph had gone too far too fast, despite their attachment to the Enlightenment. Count Pietro Verri and Gian Rinaldo Carli, who had both been presidents of the Magistrato Camerale, resigned their posts. The former wrote: 'Joseph II understood that the system was rotten, but did not understand that a simultaneous and universal destruction of the laws and practices of a country is a remedy worse than the malady. He took no account of opinion, which is also queen of the world, and made men feel all the unlimited power of a monarch who recognises no other standard than his own will' (**93**). Even so, there were no signs that the Milanese would rise in revolt.

The imposition of administrative uniformity was accompanied by an attack on the corporate status of social and economic groups within the Monarchy. Unlike many historians, Joseph did not make the mistake of supposing that privilege was a monopoly of the aristocracy. The members of the third estate fortunate enough to be masters of a guild enjoyed all manner of privileges. The most important was a monopoly of manufacture and trade in any given commodity. By means of stringent membership qualifications, the guilds had created a charmed circle of power, which an outsider found very difficult to penetrate, however skilful he may have been at his trade. Exclusiveness was only the most prominent of the guild abuses. Demarcation disputes, price-fixing, restrictive practices and xenophobia were all continually in evidence, while the quality control which had been the guilds' original justification was illusory. A more general objection was that, as separate groups with selfish interests, they were unacceptable in the unitary state demanded by enlightened political theory. In *Der Mann ohne Vorurteil* (The man without prejudice) Joseph von Sonnenfels had written:

> Society should demand only that every citizen ought to work! The permission to work is dependent on the guilds; whoever is not a member of the guild is forced to become a scoundrel. The roads to support oneself honourably are blocked. You whose function it is to punish crime, do you wonder that the prisons are crowded with criminals? . . . There are only two roads open to make one's livelihood if one does not have an inherited fortune: work or crime. The man who is denied the one path is forced to walk the other.

In 1776 Maria Theresa's ministers had produced a comprehensive scheme to break the stranglehold of the guilds but very little had been implemented. The missing vigour was supplied by Joseph after 1780. Yet even the singleminded Joseph was forced to appreciate that if all the guilds were abolished all at once, the ensuing upheaval could have brought the Monarchy to its knees. Their escape from total abolition was cold comfort for the guilds, for a series of piecemeal measures reduced them to impotent relics. Their property was confiscated and devoted to public works, their monopoly of trade was broken and the importation of foreign craftsmen forced them to review both their techniques and their prices. In 1781, for example, tanning, leatherwork and the sale of grain and bread were made free and two years later it was decreed that all journeymen with the requisite skill were to be made masters. A large number of guilds were abolished outright and even the truncated remains were placed under strict government control.

Guild control of the urban economy had been broken but towns were few and far between in the Habsburg Monarchy. In the predominantly agricultural economy, it was the subordination of peasantry to nobility that was the main obstacle in the way of the unitary state. As was explained in the previous chapter, Maria Theresa and her ministers had recognised the existence of the problem but had done precious little to solve it. By 1780 Joseph was in no mood for equivocation He had only the utmost contempt for social distinctions based on the accident of birth and took a perverse pleasure in the ostentatious display of his egalitarian sentiments. As J. C. Riesbeck observed, 'he affects simplicity and popularity almost in the extreme'. An appropriate way to annoy the Austrian nobility, which had the additional advantage of being profitable, was found in the indiscriminate sale of titles to the highest bidder. The promotion of Count Paar to the status of prince for giving 5,000 gulden to a charity was provocative enough; the ennoblement of a Jewish banker evoked violent protests based on the formidable combination of snobbery and antisemitism.

Joseph appreciated also that social caste was only a reflection of economic power; it was serfdom not convention that was the real basis of social privilege. Through his numerous tours of inspection in the provinces, the emperor was well aware of both the inhumanity of serfdom and of the damage it did to the state. He began with the abolition of personal serfdom in 1781 [**doc. 6**]. The peasant could now marry without the consent of his lord, could pursue any trade or profession and could move from one estate to another if he had fulfilled all prior obligations. For the average peasant these concessions were somewhat abstract; it was his land and the related services that concerned him most. In response to this need a series of ordinances promulgated throughout the 1780s guaranteed the peasant hereditary tenure of his property, although they did not make him outright owner. At the same time, the power of the lord to exploit his tenants through his various monopolies of milling, retailing, fishing and hunting was restricted severely. Despite these encroachments, the essential core of the lord's power remained; as long as he could exact compulsory labour services from his peasants, he would continue to control their destiny. Joseph's proposed solution would have revolutionised the Monarchy's social structure. The plan was simplicity itself—a uniform tax on land, irrespective of the social status of the owner. This was too much even for some of Joseph's faithful supporters in the bureaucracy but their master was adamant:

> One must pay no attention to the conventions and prejudices which have established themselves over the centuries. Land and soil were given to men, by nature, to succour them and they are the sole sources from which everything else derives. From this there follows the undeniable truth that only the land can satisfy the needs of the state and that no distinction can be made between the possessions of men, whatever their social status may be.

In 1784 the reluctant officials began the mammoth task of registering the ownership, size and value of every piece of property in the Monarchy. It was not until five years later that the *Kadaster* was sufficiently complete to allow the final tax decree to be published. In future the peasant was to retain 70 gulden of every 100 gulden he earned; of the remaining 30 gulden, 40 per cent was to be paid to the state and 60 per cent to the lord. That represented the sum total of the peasants' obligations; the lord could demand no labour services whatsoever. The revolutionary nature of the reform may be judged by the fact that previously the peasant retained only 30 per cent of his income. If the tax decree had been implemented fully, agricultural labour would have become prohibitively expensive, demesne farming would have become impossible, many nobles would have been impoverished and a class of free landowning peasantry would have been created. As will be shown in the final chapter, a combination of circumstances conspired to compel first the postponement and then the revocation of the decree (**84, 95, 113**).

As many contemporaries were quick to point out, Joseph's single tax on land bore a close resemblance to the *impôt unique* of the physiocrats, whose works he undoubtedly had read. His dislike of the guilds was further evidence of a liberal attitude towards economic affairs. Yet generally Joseph's economic policy defied classification. He himself said: 'As regards the financial articles of faith, I have become an atheist.' The following general statement on commerce and industry is more reminiscent of Colbert's Mercantilism than of Quesnay's Physiocracy:

> The expansion of the gross national product, with which the well-being of the subjects is so intimately connected, is impeded mainly by the preference shown for foreign goods, whose advantage over similar domestic products is often based on mere prejudice. In this way the sales of the nation's factories are restricted, the just reward of their labour is removed and the existence of the working, that is the most useful, class of society is daily made more difficult and more impossible.

Joseph's solution was typically brutal. In 1784 a tariff barrier was erected around Hungary and the Hereditary Lands to prevent the importing of almost all foreign goods. An exception was made only in the case of the Tyrol, whose economy depended on the transit trade. Even commodities unobtainable in the Monarchy, such as spices and certain raw materials, were subject to very high dues. Draconic penalties were prescribed for offenders and a network of omnicompetent customs officials was set up to apprehend them. Merchants who informed on colleagues with a criminal taste for foreign goods were rewarded. Joseph's mercantilism was not however only negative. Strenuous efforts were made to fill the commercial vacuum by encouraging indigenous enterprise through tax relief, subsidies and loans. Large sums were spent on the improvement of roads, post-stations and the Adriatic harbours. The general aim was the creation of a self-sufficient economy which made a powerful contribution to the imperial treasury through a large export surplus. In pursuit of this goal Joseph lavished as much attention on the human resources of his empire as he did on its material assets: 'I consider that the supreme object towards which the political, fiscal and even the military administrations should direct their activities is the population, that is to say the maintenance and increase of the number of subjects.' Every single citizen was duty-bound to work for the community to the best of his ability. Any attempt to evade this obligation through malingering or emigration was to be punished severely. Failed suicides were to be confined to a lunatic asylum or prison until they realised that self-preservation was a duty to God and the state, for 'the public welfare suffers harm if it becomes poorer even by one individual'. Measures were also taken against those who tried to escape by more conventional means. Without the express and expensive permission of the authorities no subject could leave the Monarchy, on pain of loss of all civil rights and confiscation of his property. In 1781, for example, officials in Bohemia were ordered to take great care lest blacksmiths escaped over the frontier into Germany. On the other hand, every possible incentive was offered to attract immigrants from other countries. Every precaution was taken to ensure that those already inside Joseph's labour camp were physically fit to make their contribution to the general welfare. The rather curious ordinances promulgated in this sphere show, if nothing else, Joseph's extraordinary attention to detail. Peasants were forbidden to drink spring water without adding vinegar first, parents were ordered to keep a careful watch to prevent their children eating poisonous roots, bathing and washing in the Danube were forbidden and girls who worked or were brought up in state institutions were forbidden to wear corsets. Presumably this last measure was ordered to enhance their child-bearing potential. Nothing illustrated more clearly the claim of the Josephist state to interfere, in the name of the whole, in every aspect of the subject's life.

The evidence available is fragmentary but it appears that Joseph's efforts were at least partially successful. He himself had no doubts; he wrote to his brother Leopold in 1786: 'Shipping on the Danube heading for the Levant and the Crimea is daily increasing. . . . Industry and manufactures are prospering in the absence of the prohibited goods. A large number of people from Nuremberg, Swabia and even from England, who used to make their living by producing in their own country, have recently settled here to carry on manufacture.' It is certain that there was a considerable increase in the number, scale and output of industrial enterprise. In Bohemia and Moravia between 1775 and 1789 the numbers employed in the woollen industry increased from 80,000 to 152,000, while the population in the same period increased by only 20 per cent (**87**). In these two provinces more than 10 per cent of the population were engaged in industry, although three-quarters of them were part-time spinners (**86**). The number of factories, as opposed to guild workshops, in Bohemia increased from 24 in 1780, to 34 in 1781, to 40 in 1782, to 63 in 1786, to 86 in 1788, to 95 in 1792. In Lower Austria too there was a comparable degree of expansion. In 1790 the great cotton factory at Schwechat near Vienna employed 45 managers or foremen, 410 masters, 1,079 journeymen, 114 apprentices,

183 labourers, 267 women and 1,208 sorters (**96**). The evidence relating to foreign trade is even less satisfactory but here again what there is suggests a considerable increase in the second half of the eighteenth century and in particular in the 1790s. One set of figures shows that the value of exports from the Hereditary Lands, with the exception of the Tyrol and the parcels of territory in south-west Germany, increased from 25·7 million gulden in 1782 to 36·7 million in 1788 (**96**). Another rough indication of the Monarchy's economic growth was the increase of the state's income from 65,777,780 gulden in 1781 to 87,483,740 gulden in 1788. The economy of Europe as a whole was expanding during this period but it would be churlish to deny the Habsburgs any of the credit for the progress of their territories. As a Czech historian has written: 'The Austrian absolute monarchy of the eighteenth century played an important role in the development of the manufacturing industry and at the same time supported the rise of new industrial relationships within the feudal order. The absolute monarchical state helped to bring about economic advance and the victory of new social relations over old ones' (**92**).

The importance of these developments, however, is largely relative. They were the harbingers of industrialisation but they were faint, hesitant and often ephemeral. In parts of Bohemia, Moravia and Upper and Lower Austria there were manufacturing establishments of considerable size but in Hungary, Styria, Carinthia, Carniola and the Tyrol the old organisation and techniques continued unchanged. Very often the 'factory'—the only but unsatisfactory translation of the German 'Fabrik'—bore no relation to its English counterpart of the same period. The principle of the division of labour was not yet fully established and most of the spinning and weaving was 'put out'. Nor was there a large entrepreneurial class. Although participation by commoners was increasing in the second half of the eighteenth century, many of the largest and most successful enterprises were founded, financed and managed by noblemen. The Bohemian Count Heinrich Franz von Rottenhan established a factory at Rothenhaus for the manufacture of cotton goods, muslin and fustian, an iron works at Kalich and a second cotton mill on another of his estates. Certainly the most enterprising of all the eighteenth-century entrepreneurs was the Emperor Francis I, acting as a private citizen. Progress had been made but to see Austria in the Josephist period as even an embryonic capitalist and industrial economy is patently absurd. An historian of industrialisation in the Habsburg Monarchy has concluded 'the artisan was still the dominant producer of industrial goods at the end of the eighteenth century' (**87**).

Reservations must also be made about the commercial expansion of the period. The tariff wall around the Hereditary Lands doubtless benefited the Austrian manufacturers but it also ruined those merchants engaged in the import trade and it provoked prompt retaliation from neighbouring countries against Austrian exporters. Complaints from the mercantile community poured in but, though they were supported by many senior officials, Joseph refused to allow any modification of his tariff system. Until the last few months of his life protests from his own subjects always strengthened rather than weakened his resolve. There is also some evidence that the tariffs failed to have the desired effect of curbing Austrian enthusiasm for foreign goods. One set of figures, the accuracy of which admittedly is open to doubt, shows that there was an export surplus in 1783 but a deficit in 1787 and 1788 (**76**).

The problems Joseph faced, however, must not be underestimated. With the exception of the very few real towns, such as Vienna and Prague, the Habsburg Monarchy was agricultural and aristocratic. Only 15 per cent of the total population lived in urban communities, only 5 per cent in towns of over 10,000. In Hungary in 1800 only 5 per cent of the population lived in towns of any kind (**96**). What little private capital there was belonged to the nobility, most of whom bought luxury goods and invested in more land but did not invest in industry. Given the social structure in rural areas, the vast majority of the population—the peasants—could play no role in the capitalist process, either as labourers or as consumers. Sandwiched between wealth and numbers was what should have been the core of Joseph's support and the class of prospective entrepreneurs. Although customarily bracketed together under the collective heading of 'bourgeoisie', they qualified for this title only in the sense that they were free citizens living in communities recognisably larger than villages. This line of argument will be developed further in the last chapter; here the simple assertion that there was no capitalist class on which Joseph could rely must suffice.

In his campaign to harness all sections of society to the communal yoke, Joseph had waged war on every kind of privilege. Yet however much he may have detested the nobility or the guilds, it was the

C

Church, the most wealthy, privileged, independent and conservative corporate institution of them all that was the prime target(**7**). There can be no doubt that personally Joseph was a pious Christian, with a sincere belief in all the essential articles of the Catholic faith. Surprised contemporaries reported that he went to confession at least every three weeks, that he expressed forcibly his contempt for heterodox opinion and that he even indulged in such quaint practices as spraying his bed with holy water. Yet although he did not share the antireligious opinions of Kaunitz, their views on the necessity of subordinating Church to state were identical [**doc. 10**]. The theories used to support Joseph's policies were in no way original; they could be found in a hundred contemporary treatises. Van Espen in the Netherlands, Muratori in Italy, von Hontheim *alias* Febronius in the Holy Roman Empire and Riegger in Austria were only the most celebrated representatives of a movement which by the 1760s had achieved what some ecclesiastical historians have described as an 'ideological revolution' in Catholic circles (**55**). The arguments most frequently used by the Josephists were summarised in two pamphlets published on the occasion of the Pope's visit to Vienna in 1782: Abbot von Rautenstrauch's *Why is Pius VI coming to Vienna?* and Johann Valentin von Eybel's *What is the Pope?* They argued that the power to bind and loose had been given by Christ to all the apostles, not just to St Peter. Consequently, every bishop was God's direct representative, everything claimed by the Pope as his exclusive prerogative could be carried out unilaterally by every bishop and papal jurisdiction did not extend beyond the boundaries of his own diocese. Furthermore, the Church as a whole had been empowered to decide on faith and morals; the Pope was obliged therefore to obey the dictates of the Councils of the Church. The Pope was head of the Church only in the sense that he was needed to preserve its unity. Rautenstrauch in particular stressed the political implications of this denial of papal authority. The bishops were to repossess the various powers usurped by the medieval popes but were to be subject in turn to the strict supervision of the secular powers: 'As he himself is a ruler and decrees what he finds to be necessary, the Holy Father knows full well that the ruler has absolute power over everything in his state, without exception. No one with the slightest knowledge of constitutional law, will deny that the clergy have no right whatsoever to form a state amongst themselves, within the state in which they live.' Eybel asserted that his opinions were based on 'healthy reason', the Bible and the Fathers of the Church but although both he and Rautenstrauch made copious references to the latter two sources, their principles were totally at odds with the ultramontanism of the papal curia. Joseph's determination to finish the work begun by Kaunitz during the previous reign made conflict inevitable.

The intensification of the anticlerical campaign came at a bad time for the papacy. Having lost its most fervent supporters by the dissolution of the Jesuit order in 1773, the curia was harried on all sides by reforming Catholic monarchs. Joseph avoided a formal schism but within two years he had created what was effectively a national Austrian Church. The publication of all papal communications required imperial permission, the nuncio was placed under strict supervision, episcopal appeals to Rome were made conditional on imperial approval, the bull against Jansenism—*Unigenitus*—was banned, all connections between Austrian monasteries and the heads of their orders resident in Rome were severed, the diocesan jurisdiction of foreign bishops which extended into Habsburg territory was excluded, the right to grant marriage dispensations was transferred from the Pope to the Austrian bishops and the bishops were compelled to swear an oath of total obedience to the secular state. The Church exchanged the domination of the Pope for the domination of the emperor. Apart from these matters of principle, Joseph became embroiled quickly in a dispute with the papacy over the conferment of benefices in the Habsburg Duchy of Milan. The need to settle this question before Joseph took unilateral action and the general feeling that Austria was moving briskly towards an open schism led Pius VI to seek a direct confrontation with the emperor. The papal visit to Vienna in March and April 1782 demonstrated three significant aspects of the struggle between Church and State: that the vast majority of the Austrian subjects detested the Josephist reforms, that Joseph was not prepared to make any real concessions and that Pius VI had no means of coercing him to do so. The Pope was even unwise enough to adopt the drastic expedient of paying a visit to *il ministro eretico*, Kaunitz. In a manner worthy of his idol Voltaire, the chancellor humiliated Pius and made him the laughing stock of enlightened Europe (**100**). Misconceived from the start, the papal expedition ended in farce.

This formal assertion of the primacy of the State was only a prelude to the internal reorganisation of the Austrian Church. Like most other reformers of the eighteenth century, Joseph turned his attention first and foremost to ecclesiastical property and in particular to the monasteries. As was emphasised in the first chapter, for the Enlightenment the monk was privilege, prejudice and fanaticism personified. Scurrilous exposés of the personal shortcomings of monks and nuns provided useful and entertaining propaganda but the reformers concentrated more on the economic, social and cultural effects of monasticism. Cesare Beccaria, whose influence was immense, had written:

> I call those politically idle, who neither contribute to the good of society by their labour, nor their riches; who continually accumulate but never spend; who are reverenced by the vulgar with stupid admiration, and regarded by the wise with disdain; who, being victims to a monastic life, and deprived of all incitement to that activity which is necessary to preserve, or increase its comforts, devote all their vigour to passions of the strongest kind, the passions of opinion (**16**).

Beccaria's remarks were particularly apposite in the context of the Habsburg Monarchy; even by contemporary standards the wealth of the monasteries was stupendous. They owned half of Carniola and at least three-eighths of Austrian Silesia and Moravia. The estates of the Carthusians alone were valued at 2,500,000 gulden. Nor could it be argued that their assets bore any real relationship to the number of members they were required to support. On dissolution the net capital of the abbey of Goldenkron in southern Bohemia amounted to over 460,000 gulden; its total complement was nineteen (**110**). Monastic patronage of the arts produced some of the finest architecture in central Europe but the sumptuous baroque of Melk or St Florian was not appreciated by the severely utilitarian Josephists.

The renewal of the amortisation laws and fresh restrictions on membership were only the opening shots in Joseph's campaign. In 1781 he ordered the dissolution of all houses belonging to contemplative orders which, he argued, served no useful purpose such as the maintenance of schools or hospitals but existed purely for the spiritual and material benefit of their inmates. This description was held to apply to 309 monasteries and 104 nunneries. Subsequent dissolutions brought the total up to 700 and the reduction of monastic personnel from 65,000 to 27,000. The redundant monks and nuns

were paid adequate pensions and, with a few exceptions, the dissolutions were conducted by the imperial officials with strict propriety.
The deserted buildings were turned into such appropriate institutions as prisons and lunatic asylums. With characteristic precipita-
tion Joseph rushed through the sale of the vast amount of property
he had accumulated. Although this inevitably depressed the prices
he obtained, more than 60 million gulden were paid into the special
fund set up 'for the benefit of religion and charity'. The monastic
houses which survived the purge were placed under strict government control, their energies being directed more towards the service
of their fellow-citizens than to the worship of their God.

Joseph's ecclesiastical policy was not simply a crude raid on the
material resources of the Church. He and his councillors were very
much concerned with the daily religious life of the common people
and in particular with the religious practices which can be grouped
under the collective heading of 'baroque piety' (**108**). Over the
centuries there had evolved a bewildering mosaic of customs which
reflected the taste of central and southern Europe for visual, sensuous and naïve forms of religious experience. During the period of
tremendous self-confidence in Austria engendered by a combination
of Counter-Reformation militancy and Prince Eugene's *Reconquista*
in the Balkans, old customs took on renewed vitality and new ones
emerged. The exuberance of the baroque art and architecture of the
period reflected not merely the whims of the aristocratic patrons but
recorded faithfully the religious aspirations of the people. The spread
of enlightened ideas among a small section of the small literate class
did nothing to dilute the enthusiasm of the vast majority for traditional forms of worship. Yet many of these inherited customs veered
uneasily across the shadowy borderline which divides true devotion
from fanaticism and superstition. In rural areas especially they were
often a curious mixture of Christianity and paganism. Predictably,
the kind of religion favoured by Christian supporters of the Enlightenment was diametrically opposed to that practised by the
populace. As Jansenism spread so did the movement for reform but
it was not until the middle of the eighteenth century that the secular
powers began to take action. In the Habsburg territories the most
important influence was that of Lodovico Muratori (1675–1750),
who wrote: 'Religious virtue, so holy and sublime in itself, ought to
hold, like all other virtues, a median position between two opposed
extremities—total lack and excess'. Published in 1747, his main work

61

on the subject—*Della regolata devozione dei Cristiani*—served as a handbook for Austrian opponents of baroque piety, although they were also influenced by French and Flemish Jansenists and by German Febronians. Under Maria Theresa a start had been made with the reduction of festivals and pilgrimages but Joseph attacked the problem with a characteristic attention to detail. The churches were purged of such 'unnecessary' accretions as dolls dressed up to depict the Virgin, relics, votive tablets, paintings and statues. Pilgrimages and processions were reduced further and finally the latter were abolished altogether. The same fate befell the lay brotherhoods, the main exponents of colourful forms of worship. In 1783 the thousands of brotherhoods were united in one nationalised institution and their energies diverted from flamboyant ceremonial to the practical assistance of their less fortunate fellow-citizens. Their confiscated property was devoted to the same end. Yet Joseph's policy was not simply destructive; precise regulations were issued governing every aspect of the religious life of the people. His Jansenist emphasis on pure devotion (*die wahre Andacht*) may have been at odds with the religious aspirations of the great majority of his subjects but did not justify accusations of indifference (**112**).

This was also shown by his attempts to raise the material and spiritual standards of the parish priests. The gross discrepancy between the upper and lower echelons of the Church was an obvious target (**99**). The enormous estates of the episcopate were secularised and their former owners reduced to the level of superior civil servants. Although considerable, the salaries of 20,000 gulden for archbishops and 12,000 gulden for bishops represented a severe contraction of their former opulence. In Hungary alone the sum of 633,000 gulden was saved annually. The parish priests benefited accordingly. In the place of their former motley collection of tithes and fees for baptisms, marriages, and burials, they were paid a regular and respectable sum by the state. Their responsibilities were also to be shared equally. With his customary enthusiasm for uniformity, Joseph ordered a redistribution of parish boundaries, based on the principle that the church should never be further away from the parishioner than an hour's walking distance. Under 'the revolutionary emperor' parishes were created at a rate ten times faster than that of his predecessors. The Josephist priest was allowed no initiative; the content and conduct of his pastoral office were dictated by the ecclesiastical commission in Vienna. To ensure his obedience the priest's training was reorganised completely. The Collegium Germanicum in Rome was closed and replaced by a new college in Pavia, in the Habsburg Duchy of Milan. The same fate befell the old theological academies in the Hereditary Lands; in their place were established the general seminaries, both the climax and the foundation of Joseph's ecclesiastical reforms. During a six-year course the young ordinands learnt a form of Catholicism which contrasted sharply with traditional scholasticism and ultramontanism. Those chiefly responsible for the new curriculum—Abbot Rautenstrauch and Provost Wittola—gave full expression to the practical Christianity favoured by their master. In particular the seminarists were to be imbued with the principle that 'the Church must be useful to the state'. They were to dispel the superstition of their flocks, encourage the peasants to employ new agricultural techniques, proclaim and recommend government ordinances from the pulpit and assist the secular officials in their implementation. The nationalisation of the clergy was perhaps the ultimate expression of the unitary state.

In pursuit of his uniform dream Joseph exceeded the bounds of political possibility. With only defective tools at his disposal, a mere exercise of will-power could not explode the entrenched forces of tradition. Yet any picture of an arrogant, intolerant and ruthless emperor trampling roughshod over the historical liberties of his subjects must be tempered by the qualification that in this period 'liberty' and 'privilege' were often regarded as synonymous. The 'liberties' of the nobles, prelates and guild masters were the correlates of the miseries of the peasants, parish priests and journeymen. The relentless emphasis on duty opened up a prospect as grim as Joseph's personality but it was service for a quite specific cause—for the material welfare of the community, not for some metaphysical concept such as God, Volk or Classless Society. Joseph was a sincere Christian who required his subjects to attend a weekly course of religious instruction, but he did not believe that life was a vale of sorrow designed to test man's suitability for admission to paradise. Nor did his state assume an Hegelian identity of its own; it remained the sum total of the individuals who composed it. The unitary state may have borne a distinct resemblance to a workhouse but at least it was a cooperative effort.

4 The Tolerant and Humane State

'La tolérance peut seule rendre la société supportable.' Voltaire's slogan of 1766 was shouted as lustily by the Austrian *Aufklärer* as it was by the philosophes. The Habsburg Monarchy had not witnessed anything as startling as the revocation of the Edict of Nantes or the Calas affair, but two centuries of religious persecution gave the reformers every reason for moral indignation. Nor had the development of the Enlightenment as an intellectual movement brought any relief to the minorities. Despite the toleration preached by her councillors, Maria Theresa was reluctant to abandon the traditional Habsburg policy of compulsory orthodoxy. She placed an embargo on the immigration of protestants, while those already in the Hereditary Lands were banished to the inhospitable regions of eastern Hungary. Some of the most violent disputes between the empress and her son were over religious persecution. In 1777, for example, it was only Joseph's threat to resign as co-regent that persuaded Maria Theresa to halt an attempt to force ten thousand Moravian protestants back into the Catholic fold at the point of the bayonet. It was clear that when Joseph was his own master toleration would be high on the list of his priorities. In a letter to Van Swieten he wrote:

> Fanaticism shall in future be known in my states only by the contempt I have for it; . . . Toleration is an effect of that beneficent increase of knowledge which now enlightens Europe, and which is owing to philosophy and the efforts of great men; it is a convincing proof of the improvement of the human mind, which has boldly reopened a road through the dominions of superstition, which was trodden centuries ago by Zoroaster and Confucius, and which fortunately for mankind, has now become the highway of monarchs (**100**).

This stirring confession of faith was implemented by the Toleration Patent of 1781. All adherents of the Lutheran, Calvinist and Orthodox denominations were allowed the private exercise of their faiths. If there were more than a hundred dissidents in any community they were permitted to build a church, although no bells were to be rung and the entrance was not to front directly on the street. They could employ a pastor and open a denominational school. Full civil equality was established; the non-Catholics were now free to buy land, to join guilds, to take degrees and to enter the civil service. Although the qualifications allowed Roman Catholicism to remain as the dominant religion in the state, an Austrian Calvinist was in a more favourable position than an English Catholic of the same period. The most immediate effect of the new patent was a large increase in the numbers of declared protestants. Within five years the total had doubled and in the Hereditary Lands alone 150 non-Catholic communities had been formed. Toleration was extended only to those calling themselves Lutheran, Calvinist or Orthodox; the various sects were excluded. A group of Bohemian Deists, who refused to subscribe to any form of Christianity, was despatched to the primitive extremities of Transylvania. Having discovered at first hand the appalling conditions there, Joseph took pity on the Deists and ordered their return to Bohemia. In future subjects declaring themselves to be Deists were to be punished with twelve strokes of the cane, not because their beliefs were wrong but because they bothered the authorities with matters they did not understand.

The practical motivation of the Toleration Patent was stated quite explicitly in its preamble which emphasised 'the harm done by any moral constraint on the one hand and of the benefit accruing for religion and the state from a true Christian toleration on the other.' Joseph hoped to emulate the success of the Prussian kings in attracting persecuted protestants to their territories, so that in 1781, for example, protestant merchants or craftsmen wishing to emigrate to Galicia were offered all manner of concessions. These included the right of public worship in six towns, exemption from all forms of personal taxation for ten years and exemption from military service. Protestant peasants settling on the royal domains were offered in addition free houses, farm buildings, tools and land. No labour services were required for six years and even then the *robot* could be commuted into a cash payment. Hope of a material gain was not however the only reason for abandoning religious persecution. Although he was accustomed to expressing himself in the uncompromising language of *raison d'état*, it is clear that Joseph believed that toleration *per se* was desirable. In the letter to Van Swieten mentioned above he wrote: 'Nobody shall any longer be exposed to hardships on account of his creed; no man shall be compelled in future to profess the religion of the state, if it be contrary to his persuasion and if he have other ideas of the right way of incurring blessedness. In future my empire shall not be the scene of abominable intolerance.'

The toleration granted to the protestants was overshadowed in terms of relative improvement by the transformation of the position of the Jews [**doc. 12**]. As elsewhere in Europe the Jewish community of the Habsburg Monarchy had been subjected periodically to pogroms and continuously to discrimination. Maria Theresa's antisemitism bordered on physical revulsion; when receiving Jewish businessmen she sat behind a screen to avoid contamination by sight. Her prejudices were shared by the great majority of her subjects but not by her son. By a series of patents in late 1781 and early 1782 Joseph freed them from the obligation of wearing a yellow Star of David on their clothes, reduced their judicial fees to the normal level, gave them the same rights of worship as those already conferred on the protestants and allowed them to found schools, to attend Christian schools and universities, to take degrees, to pursue any trade, to employ Christians as servants, to build houses where they liked in Vienna, to open factories, to engage in agriculture, to travel and settle where they liked, to visit public entertainments and to leave their homes before twelve noon on Sundays and Christian festivals. All these concessions had been denied them in the past. Compared with their co-religionists in most other European countries, the 360,000 Jews in the Habsburg territories were in an eminently favourable position, but they did not enjoy equal status with the Catholics or indeed with the protestants. Warnings from his officials that popular antisemitism might counter full toleration with a violent pogrom made Joseph cautious (**99**). It was stressed in the patents that it was not the intention of the emperor to increase the number of Jews in the state and that therefore Jewish immigrants were not to be admitted unless they brought with them some asset of exceptional value. To assuage the rabid antisemitism of the capital, Joseph ordered that no Jews were to be allowed to move to Vienna from other parts of the Monarchy without government permission and that those already there were not to form a separate communal organisation or to build a public synagogue.

Despite these qualifications, Joseph's reform was a giant step towards the total emancipation of the Jews and was recognised as such by enlightened contemporaries. The dual motivation of the concessions was made quite explicit in the preambles of the patents. Joseph stressed that in their present debased condition the Jews were unable to make a worthwhile contribution to the state. The opening of trades, professions and educational establishments was designed to assist their assimilation with the rest of the community. Displaying his usual aversion to groups, Joseph insisted that the Jews abandon their more obvious idiosyncrasies. While asserting that he did not wish to interfere in purely religious matters, he reserved the right to dictate the form and curricula of the Jewish schools. More startling was his insistence that after two years all contracts, wills, bills of exchange and accounts be drawn up in German. The use of Hebrew was to be confined to religious services and social intercourse. This emphasis on the needs of the state was typical but, as his abolition of the social humiliations imposed on the Jews by Christian bigotry showed, Joseph was motivated also by the humanitarianism of the Enlightenment. In the long and dark history of central European antisemitism the reign of Joseph II stands out as a brief flash of reason.

Together with the dissidents, the Catholic subjects benefited from Joseph's liberal attitude towards orthodoxy by his relaxation of censorship [**doc. 11**]. The efforts of Van Swieten and his colleagues in the previous reign had broken the Jesuits' monopoly, but Joseph was prepared to go much further. All matters relating to censorship, including religious publications, in all the provinces were allotted to a central commission in Vienna. The howls of protest from the Catholic hierarchy at this new encroachment by the secular power evoked only the usual curt and negative rejoinder. Acting on Joseph's instructions, the new commission adopted a remarkably liberal policy. Only pornography, aggressive atheism and superstitious tracts were banned. *Bona fide* academic research was freed from all restrictions and the import of foreign and/or protestant books was allowed. The immediate result of this liberalisation was a stream of critical books, pamphlets, plays and poems on every aspect of public life. In particular, the long-fermenting forces of anticlericalism bubbled to the surface. Eybel's series of pamphlets— *What is the Pope?*, *What is a bishop?*, *What is a priest?*, etc.—could not have been published under Maria Theresa (**100**). As Joseph remarked to the appalled Archbishop of Calocza: 'All kinds of things are being written here, and people begin to think and write more freely and intelligently'. This rather smug comment was soon overtaken by events. By the end of his reign Joseph had been forced to resort once again to the repressive policies of his predecessors.

Relaxation of censorship and religious toleration were not intended to lead to intellectual anarchy. Joseph believed that a precondition of successful communal effort in the unitary state was a uniform and practical educational system. Typical of his utilitarian attitude towards education was the following extract from an ordinance published in the first year of his reign: 'The schoolchildren should remind themselves constantly that every human being has a moral obligation to develop his intellectual powers as far as possible and that the study by which this is achieved is a duty imposed by God; that every citizen has a similar obligation to make himself capable of serving the state.' The universities suffered particularly when this principle was put into effect; they were transformed from academic institutions into factories for the production of bureaucrats. While subjects such as political science, medicine and law bloomed in the sun of imperial approval, others with less obvious practical applications, such as philosophy, withered for lack of funds. During brief and practical courses the undergraduates were imbued with Josephist principles and the administrative techniques required for their implementation. A similar situation prevailed in the grammar schools. With his customary contempt for the cultivation of the individual, Joseph stressed that there should be no overproduction of intellectuals. To ensure this, school fees of 12 gulden per annum were charged, with the predictable result that numbers attending grammar schools declined sharply. All schools which did not conform to the Josephist ideal were ordered to be closed; 813 perished on this account. After 1783 all reading primers in use in rural schools were to include the duties owed by the subject to his ruler. With some justification Mirabeau exclaimed: 'Great God! He even wants to put the souls in uniform! That is the summit of despotism!'

Yet although Joseph despised intellectual endeavour for its own sake and higher education suffered accordingly, he did a great deal to improve the primary schools. Many hundreds of new ones were created, their teachers were paid proper salaries and every attempt was made to compel attendance. Parents whose children attended regularly were rewarded financially, while those who kept their children at home were fined. Also unusual, in an eighteenth-century context, was the emphasis on the need to educate women. The Josephist educational system may have been designed to produce faceless automatons but in 1790 relatively there were more children of school age actually attending school than in any other country in continental Europe. It must also be remembered that, however anti-intellectual it may appear to the twentieth century, Joseph's system was 'enlightened' in the sense that it was influenced strongly by pedagogues such as Felbiger [**doc. 3**].

Religious toleration and the relaxation of censorship made the Habsburg Monarchy more acceptable for protestants, Jews and intellectuals of any religion; all subjects benefited from his judicial reforms (**99**). As in so many other cases, Joseph acted as the political executor of his mother. Maria Theresa had made an attempt to reform the laws and legal institutions but the results had been incomplete and unsatisfactory. Influenced as he was by Beccaria, Sonnenfels and Martini, Joseph was prepared to go much further. In the Hereditary Lands few structural alterations were required, but in the other provinces a great deal remained to be done. In Hungary, for example, cases were dubbed 'immortal' by despairing litigants and the supreme court of appeal was in recess for nine months in the year. Everywhere Joseph established a uniform system of appeal, staffed the courts with professionals accountable to the central authorities in Vienna, took the division of the administration from the regular political administration one stage further and by means of new procedural regulations made the course of justice quicker and cheaper. Some qualifications must be made. Administrative bodies retained some judicial functions, lack of trained personnel robbed the reforms of much of their impact and in civil jurisdiction complete equality between the social classes was not achieved. Nor did the codification of the civil laws, begun hesitantly during the previous reign, make any appreciable progress during the 1780s (**104**). The major innovations related to marriage, which was demoted from its sacramental status to that of a civil contract. The right of dispensing from Catholic matrimonial regulations was transferred from Rome to the Austrian episcopacy and interdenominational marriages were allowed. More startling was the admission of divorce in cases of impotence, adultery, criminal conviction or desertion. In the sphere of civil jurisdiction Joseph's achievement was comparable with that of Frederick the Great and Cocceji in Prussia.

The influence of enlightened jurisprudence was more marked in Joseph's attitude towards crime and punishment. The Criminal Code published in 1787 introduced both reason and humanity to the confused and barbaric penal system. The most advanced stipulation of the new code, which applied uniformly to all provinces of the Monarchy, was clause twenty, which decreed: 'No person shall be punished with death, except in cases in which it shall be pronounced according to law in a court-martial.' Barbaric penalties such as mutilation were abolished. Joseph's rejection of any clerical influence on law enforcement was shown by his refusal to treat mortal sins as major crimes. Magic and witchcraft, hitherto capital crimes, were now placed in the same category as fraud. Similarly enlightened was the attention paid to the question of responsibility: lunatics, drunks and children were exonerated. Great emphasis was laid on speed; a suspect had to be formally charged within twenty-four hours of his arrest and brought before a court for a preliminary hearing within three days. A further advance was the establishment of remand prisons for those refused bail. The qualifications made about the reforms of civil law do not apply to the Criminal Code: justice was severed completely from political administration and equality before the law was established. The sight of a baron, dressed in prison garb and his head shaven, sweeping the streets, was perhaps the most graphic illustration of Joseph's contempt for social conventions. All these innovations would have won the approbation of Voltaire or Montesquieu but other aspects would have met only with censure [**doc. 2**]. The public was not admitted to criminal trials and the accused had no defender. Capital punishment was abolished but was replaced by penal servitude of extreme ferocity. The exertions of pulling barges up and down the Danube meant usually that the criminal's reprieve was only temporary. Joseph von Sonnenfels justified this brutality with the argument that 'severe, sustained and public labour makes punishment useful for the state', but few theorists shared his exclusive utilitarianism. Nevertheless, in a century in which an English child could be hanged for stealing five shillings and a French adolescent could have his tongue cut out, his right hand cut off and be burned at the stake for uttering some childish blasphemies, Joseph II was a model of rationality.

Humanity and reason were reflected also in Joseph's attitude towards those subjects reduced to destitution through no fault of their own (**112**). Before Joseph's reforms, welfare services in the Habsburg territories were left to the haphazard attentions of the Church and private bodies. Although they had achieved a great deal, there were many obvious deficiencies. In Prague, for example, a city with over 60,000 inhabitants, there were only a hundred beds for sick males at the house of the Merciful Brethren and only forty-eight beds for sick females at the convent of St Elisabeth. The mentally ill suffered particularly from neglect; if there were rooms they were sent to hospital but more usually they were confined in prison. The blind, crippled and deaf mute were left to fend for themselves. Following the Jansenist emphasis on practical charity and simple devotion, many enlightened Catholic publicists agreed that the Church should devote less of its resources to lavish ceremonial and more to the relief of the less fortunate members of its flock. The most important single publication of this school was Muratori's *Concerning Christian Charity*, first published in Italy in 1723 and translated into German in 1761.

What the Church declined to give voluntarily, Joseph was prepared to extract by force. Of the enormous sum raised by the dissolution of the monasteries, much was devoted to the provision of proper welfare services. More funds became available when the hundreds of lay brotherhoods were amalgamated and their assets confiscated. Those in Lower Austria yielded 1,600,000 gulden and those in Bohemia almost another million. The capital thus assembled was administered by a special commission set up under the chairmanship of the Bohemian philanthropist Count Johann Buquoy. Within a few years the commission had founded orphanages, foundling homes, hospitals, maternity hospitals, medical academies and institutions for unmarried mothers, the blind, the deaf mute and the lunatic. By 1785 the Vienna General Hospital had two thousand beds. A sliding-scale of charges was established, but paupers were admitted free.

The urban population was not the only beneficiary of the new system. Joseph's instructions to the district commissioners in 1784 included the obligation to observe 'whether anyone cared for the orphans, foundlings and homeless children. Whether anything was being done for the blind, deaf and crippled children to make them ultimately self-supporting. . . . Whether the church penances and the dishonouring punishments of unfortunate girls were abolished, and whether there were institutions for the saving of such girls and foundlings.' It was impressed on surgeons, doctors and midwives that they were obliged 'by the highest laws and by their oath to come to the aid of the truly poor at all times'. Peasants reduced to destitution by ill-health were to receive free medicine, treatment and food, one-third of the cost being met by their lords and the other two-thirds by the state. Few qualifying remarks need to be made about this aspect of Joseph's legislative activity, which too often has been neglected by historians. Most European countries had to wait until well into the twentieth century before a similar system of public welfare was established. A healthy subject was of course more useful than a sick one but the influence of contemporary enlightened theory is unmistakable. All members of the reconstituted brotherhood were to be provided with a copy of Muratori's *Reflections on the abolition of begging and the maintenance of the poor*. It is patently absurd to suggest that considerations of state power were of primary importance: not even Joseph II could have hoped to transform a deaf and dumb blind crippled lunatic illegitimate unmarried mother into an effective fighting-unit.

5 Problems

As he lay on his deathbed early in 1790, Joseph composed his own bitter epitaph: 'Here lies Joseph II, who was unfortunate in all his enterprises.' A reign he had begun in a mood of impatient optimism ended in an atmosphere invoked by acute physical suffering and mental depression. During the last few years disaster followed disaster. Belgium appeared to be lost for ever, Hungary was on the verge of open insurrection and everywhere opposition from all sections of society had forced the abandonment of much of the Josephist reform programme. In the Balkans the campaigns against the Turks began to make headway only when Joseph resigned over-all direction. That the reign ended with an ineradicable taint of failure was due not only to the insuperable problems he faced but also to his personal shortcomings.

Of all the problems the most intractable proved to be the provincialism which had plagued successive generations of Habsburgs. Opposition from the Magyars, Belgians or Italians, distinguished from the centre by differences of language and culture was only to be expected but Joseph also succeeded in provoking the population of the Hereditary Lands (**99**). The reaction to his attempts to create a unitary state showed that most of his subjects still placed loyalty to their province before loyalty to the whole. As a Tyrolean nobleman wrote:

What does it concern the people of the Tyrol what happens in Bohemia, Moravia and other countries? The Tyrolese have their own sovereign, their own laws, their own constitution, and their own country. It is a matter of pure accident that their prince also happens to rule over other countries. They are flattered, of course, that they have a prince-protector who is a great monarch and rules over numerous provinces, but they do not wish to pay for their honour by the loss of their fundamental laws, which are guaranteed to them by God and the estates alike.

73

Joseph II as Sole Ruler (1780-90)

The difference between impoverished and backward Carinthia and the Tyrol, with its prosperous and independent free peasants, or Lower Austria, the economic centre of the Monarchy which included the 240,000 inhabitants of Vienna, were felt to be more important than the similarities. The Province, the best but still unsatisfactory translation of the German word *Land*, was far more than a mere territorial division. The *Land* was also the sum total of the political, social and economic relationships within that territory. However idiosyncratic, the traditional way of life was regarded as being immutable; the law was quite simply the *status quo*. As one recent historian has expressed it: '*Land* was therefore a concrete socio-political situation, sanctified by law within a territorial unit' (**104**). Any idea that the state could claim a monopoly of public authority and alter the traditional structure was quite repugnant to those inhabitants of the *Land* of any political importance. Maria Theresa's cautious centralisation had been irritating enough; Joseph's radical assault on provincial privileges evoked violent protests. Particularly unpopular was the attempt to impose a uniform judicial system on the Hereditary Lands, for the sanctity of customary legal processes was an essential component of the concept of *Land*. Inevitably, it was the tax decree, with its revolutionary political, social and economic implications, which provoked the most determined opposition. Even the Lower Austrian estates, normally models of docility, as a result of residence in Vienna and imperial patronage, made tremulous noises of protest. The incessant remonstrances of the various estates were rejected by Joseph with contempt and there is no evidence that they were prepared to resort to force of arms. Nevertheless, the continued vitality of provincial loyalties contributed to Joseph's need to make concessions at the end of his reign and to the further dismantling of his system after his death.

In terms of decibels the complaints of the Hereditary Lands were mere whimpers when compared with the volume of protest which issued from Hungary. The Magyar gentry maintained a roar of disapproval throughout the reign. These were men who knew the Tripartitum—the codification of Hungarian law—off by heart and were not prepared to accept the slightest modification of the *status quo* (**62**). Joseph could destroy the structure of the county assemblies but he could not destroy their spirit and in the end, of all his subjects, it was the Hungarian nobles who extracted the most far-reaching concessions. Relations between them and their emperor were bedevilled by the perennial problem of Hungary's privileged fiscal position. Of the twenty million gulden raised there, only a fifth was sent to Vienna; the remainder was used for purely local purposes. From the six million inhabitants of the Hereditary Lands the central treasury collected eighteen million gulden in revenue, while from the three million inhabitants of Hungary it collected only four million gulden (97). All attempts to redress the balance had been thwarted by the understandable opposition of the Hungarian parliament and the county assemblies. With some justification the Habsburgs retaliated by treating the kingdom as a colony. The tariff wall they erected allowed the country to be only a source of cheap raw materials, and reserved for Austrian merchants a monopoly of trade in manufactured articles. Hungarian industry was kept in a depressed state as an act of deliberate policy. With his customary thoroughness Joseph II turned the mercantilist screws even tighter. When the Chancellery made a number of proposals to assist development there, Joseph rejected them with the words: 'Until Hungary is placed in a position equal to that of the other Hereditary Provinces, the Treasury cannot support any handicraft which would curtail the means of subsistence of the Hereditary Provinces.' These mutual grievances fed on each other, friction was constant, compromise impossible.

Unlike their colleagues in the Hereditary Lands the Magyar nobles did not shrink from the prospect of armed insurrection. Such measures as the administrative reorganisation took them to the brink of insurrection; the tax decree, had it been enforced, would have taken them over it. Denied any constitutional means of protest by Joseph's abolition of the county assemblies and failure to summon the parliament, the Hungarians reached for their swords. In 1788 and 1789, as the land survey preceding the new tax scheme drew to a close, signs proliferated that a national revolt was imminent (99). Appeals were even made to King Frederick William II of Prussia for assistance against the Habsburgs. Informed of the danger through the sometimes imaginative reports of his spies, even the single-minded Joseph was compelled to appreciate the need for concessions. With the war against the Turks going badly, an insurrection behind his own lines could have brought disaster. There were no effective allies in Hungary he might have used to keep the nobles quiet. The towns, which were inhabited mainly by German-speaking citizens loyal to Vienna, were few, small and scattered. Ironically the Habsburgs' discrimination against Hungarian industry now militated against them; the total population of the royal free boroughs in 1787 was only 402,000, including the nobility and clergy who lived there. The subject Slav races, whose hatred of the Magyars was exploited so efficiently in the nineteenth century, were not yet sufficiently aware of their separate identity. Finally, not even Joseph was prepared to appeal over the heads of the nobles to the peasants. The first stage in the retreat came at the end of 1789 when he agreed to summon the Hungarian parliament, last convened by Maria Theresa in 1765. On 28 January 1790, three weeks before he died, Joseph revoked his administrative reforms. This marked the end of the first and last really determined attempt to make Hungary just another Habsburg province. As a contemporary poet rejoiced:

> What rapture, what bliss
> Arrest the course of discontent!
> The sun of golden freedom
> Rises again over this land.
> With its rays it banishes
> The night of all the innovations
> And seeks to refresh everyone.

As one of Leopold II's first actions was to suspend and then abandon the tax decree, the Hungarian nobles had established once again their predominant political and social position.

Joseph bought peace in Hungary at the price of abandoning much of his programme but he proved unable to prevent open revolution breaking out in Belgium (**72**) [**doc. 15**]. The Austrian Habsburgs had governed the province only since the Treaty of Utrecht of 1713 and the Belgians had had little time to accustom themselves to the idea of accepting orders from distant Vienna. In the clerical and conservative atmosphere which prevailed there in 1780 bitter opposition to Joseph's reforms was entirely predictable. In 1787 passive resistance made way for overt acts of civil disobedience, with serious riots in Brussels. Joseph responded by sending Count Trauttmansdorff and General d'Alton as the new plenipotentiary minister and military commander respectively, with instructions to adopt a hard line against the dissidents. At the same time he summoned deputies of the Belgian provincial estates to Vienna to discuss their grievances, but no compromise could be found. During the next two years confusion reigned; sporadic insurrections were countered by repression, which in turn fostered further demonstrations. The feud between Trauttmansdorff and d'Alton, the vacillating attitude of Joseph and the diversion of military resources to the war against the Turks all contributed to the steady erosion of the Austrian position. Large numbers of Belgians escaped into the United Provinces or the Prince-Bishopric of Liège—which itself had just ejected its ruler—and there made preparations for the liberation of their country. In October 1789 an army of Belgian patriots which entered from the north defeated d'Alton's forces. With the assistance of popular insurrections throughout the country, the invaders succeeded in ejecting all the Austrian troops (**106**). The triumphant rebels renounced their allegiance to the Habsburgs and declared the United States of Belgium. The province appeared to be lost for ever.

While not comparable with Silesia in terms of value, the loss of Belgium was a terrible blow. The spectacle of ill-armed irregulars running the professional Austrian legions out of the province was an intolerable humiliation. The beleaguered Joseph's reaction was that of despair mixed with bewilderment: 'I do not understand why, against whom, how, nor for what all this is directed.' He could not believe that his subjects would spurn measures which were clearly in their own best interests. This incredulity indicated a major flaw in Joseph's political make-up—intellectual arrogance [**doc. 17**]. His belief in his own infallibility and his failure to appreciate that men will not always prefer what is rational to what is merely traditional led him to misunderstand entirely the strength and the nature of the Belgian opposition. The nobles and priests, whose political, social and economic power was threatened by Joseph's measures, found it easy to persuade the mass of the people that the reform programme was the work of an Anti-Christ. The extent to which clerical conservatism permeated every section of society was shown by developments after the expulsion of the Austrians. The great majority of Belgians merely wished to restore the *status quo* prevailing before Joseph began his reforms. A group of radicals which sought to make the political institutions democratic was hounded out of the country by a genuinely popular 'white terror'. There were latent divisions within Belgian society which Joseph might have exploited but, by trying to make a clean sweep of all institutions simultaneously, he succeeded only in alienating all of the people all at once.

This failure to overcome provincial loyalties is not only explicable in terms of their remarkable tenacity and Joseph's misguided tactics;

it was due also to the shortcomings of the central authorities. In Vienna there were numerous dedicated Josephist officials who believed passionately in the emperor's reforms and strove to implement them. At a local level there was little enthusiasm and less ability. Yet a precondition for the success of the Josephist state, with its encyclopaedic responsibilities, was a loyal and efficient bureaucracy. Joseph himself had a quite unremitting view of the obligations incumbent on an official. Referring to the circle captains (*Kreishauptleute*), he wrote:

> They must devote all their energies to the imperial service zealously and untiringly, every hour and day of the week they must think only of their service, they must tour their districts diligently, must observe everything vigilantly and must send a precise report about it to the provincial authorities; and in the execution of these duties they must never flag, physically or mentally.

Every effort had been made to assist the officials in living up to these high ideals. The educational system, for example, had been remodelled to provide them with the requisite knowledge. Nepotism and social distinctions had been abolished; everyone had been required to start at the bottom. A purge of corrupt and incompetent officials at the beginning of the reign had sought to establish new standards of professional integrity. Constant supervision was maintained to ensure that there was no deviation from the Josephist ideal: every year high officials were required to send in reports on the length of service, family circumstances, wealth, diligence, knowledge, ability, character and failings of their subordinates. There was even a rubric which ran 'Does he lead a pious Christian life?' [**doc. 9**].

The attempt to create a bureaucracy worthy of Joseph's reform programme failed miserably. A Swiss traveller echoed the views of many observers when he wrote: 'Though eminent men are the head of the several authorities [in Vienna], the general character of the imperial officials is proportionately the more contemptible. As a rule there is not a spark of patriotism in them; they know nothing, are disagreeable and are not even hard-working. For them the main point is the salary and the title—the work is a minor matter.' The mediocrity of the Austrian official was attributable in part to a lack of incentive; his lot was signally unhappy. He was expected to work very long hours at low rates of pay, while the slightest misdemeanour was heavily punished, by reduction of salary, dismissal without a pension or by imprisonment. Vilified by the public as a result of the unpopular measures he was compelled to enforce, he was denied even material rewards. An anonymous pamphlet of 1783 claimed that many officials faced destitution. In these circumstances it is not surprising that Joseph's bureaucracy did not attract the most dedicated or talented of men (**99**). Their enthusiasm for their work was not enhanced by their subjection to an incessant volume of abuse from their emperor [**doc. 7**]. Joseph must have been aware that not everyone was as industrious or as fanatically devoted to the public welfare as he was but his standards were inflexible. Public reference to his officials as 'these hired lackeys', or comments such as 'Taken as a whole, the so-called officials here are the kind of people who are better suited to sweeping the street than to affairs of state', did nothing to improve morale. Neither did the knowledge that Count Pergen's secret police had orders to spy on officials, or the decree which promised pecuniary rewards to those who spied on their colleagues. Distrusted and badly paid by their employer, the officials found it difficult to resist the temptation to come to terms with the local establishment and to resist passively the orders issuing from Vienna. In Hungary, where central control was even more illusory, the supposedly imperial officials collaborated with the local gentry in the sabotage of the reforms.

The hostility of those who should have been his firmest allies indicated the extent to which Joseph's radicalism had led to self-imposed isolation. For there were no other groups within his state to whom he might have appealed. The traditional bastions of the Habsburg Monarchy—the nobility and the Church—had a strong vested interest in the *status quo* and almost by definition were opposed to the Josephist programme. The inhabitants of the towns were relatively few in number and were often as conservative as their social superiors. To have appealed direct to the peasants would have been to court social anarchy. The inefficiency and disloyalty of the bureaucracy can of course be overdramatised. There were some officials, some nobles and even some bishops who supported Joseph, but in the welter of prescriptive rights that was the Habsburg Empire they were voices crying in the wilderness. A new generation of officials and priests, trained in the reformed schools, universities and seminaries, might have proved more cooperative but time was one thing not susceptible to the demands of reason. As Joseph lamented to his brother Leopold: 'There is an absolute lack of men who can conceive and will; almost no one is animated by zeal for the good of the fatherland; there is no one to carry out my ideas.'

Even had there been officials of suitable calibre available, Joseph would still have had to contend with the paradoxical opposition of the intended beneficiaries. The emperor and his subjects held sharply diverging opinions as to what was best for the latter. Popular conservatism is a phenomenon which has not attracted the attention it deserves, perhaps because change is inevitably more interesting than stability, but it was very much a reality in the Habsburg Empire at the end of the eighteenth century. Except in times of acute economic crisis, the preindustrial social ethos was essentially static. Behind this conservatism there lurked of course a great deal of prejudice, superstition and self-interest but there was also the feeling, however incoherently expressed, that the traditional political, judicial, social, economic and religious fabric should not be tampered with by the central authorities. In the Roman Catholic provinces of the Monarchy this found its most vocal expression in resistance to the Josephist religious policies. The Jansenist movement discussed in an earlier chapter affected only a tiny minority of the population; the great majority remained fervently attached to traditional forms of worship (**112**) [**doc. 14**]. Even in Vienna, the most cosmopolitan city in the Monarchy, there was vehement opposition to the reforms. In a book about the city published in 1789, Joseph Pezzl wrote that the most unpopular of all the innovations were the toleration granted to the heretics and Jews, the dissolution of the monasteries, the ban on church music, the abolition of a number of traditional services and the removal of dolls dressed up to depict various saints [**doc. 13**].

Throughout his empire, Joseph's legislation was studiously ignored. Where determined attempts were made to enforce it, open violence often resulted. In Bregenz in the Tyrol, for example, a mob tore down an imperial decree relating to changes in the liturgy, assaulted the commissar and forced the local official and priest to sign a declaration that the Mass would be celebrated in the old way. In many areas the peasants formed armed bands to defend their beloved statues against attempts by the imperial officials to remove them. Perhaps the most convincing demonstration of the common people's solidarity with the old religious order came when the Pope visited Vienna in 1782. The British ambassador reported:

> The eagerness of the common people to receive his benediction amounted to a frenzy. The course of the Danube was fairly choked by the crowd of boats which bore the floods of pious pilgrims, and the great market place was often found filled with shoes and hats lost in the scuffle by the assembled multitudes; also, by twenty or thirty thousand (some say 50,000) at a time, passed into the streets to the Imperial palace, at the balcony of which, repeatedly during the day, its illustrious guest was obliged to show himself, and distributed blessings to successive shoals of devotees (**100**).

Joseph was no more impressed by the demonstrations of his subjects than he was by the protests of Pius VI and made no concessions to their conservatism. Nevertheless, in the short term their passive resistance obstructed the implementation of the reforms and in the long term their vociferous protests persuaded Joseph's successors to abandon his programme.

Popular opposition was not confined to the religious policies. Caroline Pichler, a contemporary *littérateuse*, recorded that a great number of people believed that every innovation was by definition heretical (**10**). This opposition of the non-nobles was based of course on more than irrational superstition. As was emphasised in an earlier chapter, privilege was by no means the monopoly of the aristocracy. Thus the attempt to break the guilds' control of the economy collided with as many vested interests as the fiscal or administrative reforms. The guild-masters, together with the journeymen and apprentices who aspired to become masters, resented bitterly the abolition of their privileges, the confiscation of their collective property and the importing of foreign craftsmen. The merchants detested the new restrictions on imports and the transit trade and the chicaneries of the omnicompetent customs officials. The townspeople in general were opposed to their reduction to the same level as the rural inhabitants. Many towns owned landed estates and joined the nobility in their opposition to the abolition of seignorial rights. The abrogation of their rights of self-administration aroused similar resentment. A good example of their corporate consciousness is the following extract from a remonstrance of the urban Saxons of Transylvania: 'Just as the nobleman sees his privilege in the fact that he is not confused with his subjects, so the free Saxon, supported by his constitution, does not wish to be placed in the same whipping-category as the peasants.'

As they had so very little to lose, this 'whipping-category' might have been expected to provide the emperor with some much-needed support, but even the peasants raised objections to the Josephist programme. Their complaints centred on the new conscription system. As a result of the various exemptions, only day-labourers and the poorer peasants were liable for military service, which in Joseph's army was a life sentence. In some provinces the unsavoury techniques of the recruiting sergeants combined with these grievances to provoke open resistance. Boundary marks dividing the cantons were torn down, recruiting parties were ejected by force, thousands of young men escaped into neighbouring countries and complaints poured in from the estates that the economy was suffering irreparable harm. The peasants were also of course among the most virulent opponents of the religious and educational reforms. Despite the unpopularity of these measures, it is clear that the peasants were Joseph's most enthusiastic supporters. The policies designed to transform them from servile dependants into free landowners convinced them that he represented their only hope of material advancement. On his death many villages erected crude monuments to his memory and contemporaries reported that his picture could be found in many rural hovels. Yet, as was emphasised earlier in a different context, the peasants could not save Joseph from the opposition of privilege and bureaucratic inefficiency.

Tenacious provincialism, unresponsive tools and intractable subject matter—all three were to a large extent beyond Joseph's control but in one respect he could not evade personal responsibility for his failure. His misguided enthusiasm for martial glory led to one catastrophe after another in foreign affairs and ultimately was responsible for the domestic crisis at the end of the reign. For Joseph was an inept diplomat and a worse soldier. The combination of reckless ambition, limited resources and feeble resolution was not the ideal recipe for diplomatic success. As Joseph swaggered and bullied his way across the European stage he convinced no one but himself. An ominous demonstration of his limitations came while he was still only co-regent, with the Bavarian War of Succession (**83, 107**). In 1777 the Elector Maximilian Joseph of Bavaria died, leaving no legitimate offspring; his heir was therefore the head of a collateral branch of the Wittelsbach family, the Elector Karl Theodor of the

Palatinate. For some time Joseph had been negotiating to acquire
Bavaria in exchange for Belgium but now he thought he saw an
opportunity to annex part of the electorate at no cost to himself.
The tenuous genealogical claims he laid were recognised for the pretext that they were. More convincing was his immediate invasion.
Blinded by his pursuit of glory, Joseph failed to appreciate that the
European Powers could not ignore this act of piracy, which would
have tilted the balance of power decisively in Austria's favour. In
particular, his casual disregard of even the more superficial conventions of international relations allowed Frederick the Great to
emerge in the improbable guise of defender of the Holy Roman
Empire. Frederick had no difficulty in foiling Joseph's attempts to
gain international recognition of his seizure of Bavaria and by a
show of force he compelled Joseph to come to terms. From the
summer of 1778 to the spring of the following year the Prussian and
Austrian armies marched and countermarched up and down
Bohemia but never actually met on the field of battle. Finally Joseph
was induced by French and Russian pressure to sign the peace of
Teschen (13 May 1779), by which Bavaria passed to Karl Theodor
of the Palatinate and Austria received the meagre consolation prize
of a small strip of territory on the river Inn. The latter's thirty-four
square miles had been purchased at a cost of seriously depleted
financial reserves, the devastation of large areas of Bohemia and the
tarnishing of Joseph's reputation as diplomat and soldier. The whole
sorry affair did not deserve the grandiose title 'War of Bavarian
Succession'; more appropriate was that coined by the common
soldiers actually engaged: 'The Potato War'.

Maria Theresa had acted as a restraining influence during this
episode, but after her death Joseph was given full rein to indulge his
taste for foreign adventure. In 1782 border incidents between Belgium and the United Provinces gave him the opportunity to attempt
to force the opening of the river Scheldt, closed to Belgian commerce
de facto since the beginning of the seventeenth century and *de jure*
since the Treaty of Westphalia of 1648. Yet without an adequate navy
to enforce his claim, Joseph was reduced to purely verbal aggression.
Again, he had started an international dispute he could not finish.
Kaunitz appreciated the futility of the exercise but his influence on
the emperor had waned. After some inconclusive skirmishing and a
great deal of negotiation the affair was finally settled by the Peace
of Fontainebleau in 1785. Although Austria received ten million

gulden from the Dutch as compensation, the Scheldt remained closed. Joseph's inability to support his martial rhetoric with effective action had been exposed yet again.

Joseph's handling of these two incidents had shown all the finesse of a rogue elephant; the same lack of tact was apparent in his policy towards the Holy Roman Empire. Although Habsburg sovereignty over its component states was purely nominal, their support or at least neutrality was essential. Disregarding all the advice of Kaunitz, Joseph only succeeded in uniting against him a formidable coalition. At the beginning of 1785 rumours proliferated that the plan to exchange Belgium for Bavaria had been resurrected. They were right; Joseph had clearly learnt nothing from the 'Potato War' fiasco. The opposition of France and the heir of the current Elector of Bavaria doomed the project from the start and in addition Frederick the Great was given another opportunity to demonstrate that Prussia had replaced Austria as the dominant power in Germany. Already alarmed by his numerous contraventions of the imperial constitution, the German princes were reminded by his bid for Bavaria of the attempts of Charles V and Ferdinand II to establish Habsburg hegemony in the Empire. Frederick channelled this fear and resentment into his 'League of Princes', which was founded in the summer of 1785. Prussia, Hanover, Saxony, Mainz and fourteen other less important states joined. Most indicative of the chaos wrought by Joseph's muscular but mindless foreign policy was the defection of the Archbishop-Elector of Mainz, who was the Roman Catholic primate, the arch-chancellor of the Empire and traditionally one of the Habsburgs' most loyal supporters. The League of Princes was a major milestone on the road which led to Königgrätz.

As Kaunitz watched the goodwill he had built up over decades being dissipated in months, he withdrew increasingly from the conduct of affairs. He lamented to the Austrian minister in Belgium, Count Trauttmansdorff: 'You know just as I do how much this wretched man [Joseph] deserves the title of infamy "all-time destroyer of the Empire".' Relations between the emperor and his chancellor deteriorated to the extent that they did not meet during the last two years of Joseph's life. It may be doubtful whether Kaunitz commented 'That was good of him' when he heard that Joseph had died, but it is certain that he wrote on his return from the funeral that he had approached the emperor with a feeling of relief for the first time for many years. This bitterness was not just senile malice; in the international sphere Joseph had been a disaster for Austria [**doc. 17**].

One reason for Joseph's failure to reopen the Scheldt and to acquire Bavaria had been the opposition of his nominal ally France. The disruption of this alliance, which had lasted since Kaunitz's 'diplomatic revolution' of 1756, was largely Joseph's responsibility. It should have been clear that the French could never have allowed the Habsburgs to take even the smallest step in the direction of hegemony in Europe. As he had succeeded in alienating almost every other European power of any importance, Joseph was forced to rely increasingly on the support of Russia (**81**). In 1781 a defensive alliance was concluded between the two countries, aimed primarily at the partition of the Ottoman Empire. It was clear from the start that Russia would be the main beneficiary, for although there was little that Catherine the Great could do for Joseph in western Europe, there was a great deal that he could do to assist her drive to Constantinople. This became clear when Joseph began his last and most catastrophic foreign adventure in 1787. After the Turkish declaration of war on Russia in the summer of that year, he proved eager to fulfil his treaty obligations. At the head of an army 200,000 strong, he marched into Ottoman territory without bothering to observe the formality of declaring war. His insistence on directing the campaign personally led only to a thorough exposure of his limitations as a military commander. Decimated by a terrible epidemic and demoralised by feeble leadership, the Austrian armies retreated, allowing the Turks to devastate southern Hungary. It was not until the dying Joseph returned to Vienna at the end of 1788, leaving Marshal Loudon in charge, that the situation began to improve (**100**). His successor Leopold recognised the futility of the war and brought it to an abrupt halt. After three years of fighting the Austrians had gained precisely nothing. Russia, on the other hand, secured recognition of her annexation of the Crimea, advanced her south-western frontier to the river Dniester and thus placed herself in an admirable position for the domination of the Balkans. As events in the nineteenth century were to show, the feeble Turks were better neighbours for the Habsburgs than the aggressive Russians.

Joseph's misfortunes in the field of foreign policy cannot be divorced from his domestic failures. In view of the problems already discussed, radical reform at home and aggression abroad were incompatible. With his military resources committed to the fruitless war against the Turks, Joseph was unable to deal with his domestic enemies. Belgium went by default, while Hungary was saved only at a cost of important concessions. Although it is impossible to prove, it also seems likely that the humiliations Joseph suffered in his foreign policy made his domestic programme correspondingly less attractive to his subjects. Nor did the various campaigns bring any material benefit to his country. The scrap of territory ceded by Bavaria and the 10 million gulden squeezed from the Dutch represented derisory compensation for the enormous outlay involved. In 1786, one of the few years in which Joseph managed to keep his hands off his neighbours' property, the accounts of the Monarchy showed a small credit balance. This encouraging development was strangled by the Turkish War. By the end of 1789 the annual deficit had soared to 22 million gulden and the National Debt stood at 400 million. Contemporary observers were dismayed not so much by his lack of success as by his lack of scruple. To them he appeared as a schizophrenic: a champion of the Enlightenment in his own country but an unprincipled thug outside it. The French Physiocrat Du Pont wrote:

> The Emperor is hard to judge. When one observes what he has done and is doing daily for his country, he is a prince of the rarest merit. . . . But on the other hand when one takes a look at his political attitude towards his neighbours, his avidity for war, his desire for aggrandisement, the partition of Poland, the invasion of Bavaria, the plots against the Turkish Empire, his disrespect for old treaties, his inclination to decide everything by force, then the noble-minded eagle is only a terrible bird of prey (**26**).

Ultimately, all the raids of the predator could not efface the memory of the eagle's legislative achievements. As the Prussian general Moltke wrote in 1831: 'This Austrian emperor, to whom history still owes rehabilitation, attempted to achieve by means of the authority and power vested in him, what the French Revolution only obtained after many years of blood and terror.' With some justification, Joseph is often referred to as 'the revolutionary emperor'. It was ironic therefore that towards the end of his reign he should face yet another challenge, this time from a group of dissidents who believed that he was not radical enough (**III**). In the critical atmosphere engendered by the relaxation of censorship, the educational reforms and the attacks on privilege, it was inevitable that Joseph's principle of 'everything for the people but nothing by the people' would not meet with universal approval. As the publicists hastened to take advantage of the emperor's belief in freedom of expression, Vienna was deluged with pamphlets criticising every aspect of public life. The way was also opened for the import of the more radical products of the French Enlightenment. Many of these works, domestic or foreign, did not rise above the level of crude pornography or scurrilous libel but some had to be taken seriously (**100**). Joseph could shrug off personal attacks with contempt, but he was less amused by charges that his reforms were inadequate. Some radicals, for example, demanded that religious toleration be made indiscriminate and unconditional, while others called for the total abolition of the nobility, who 'ruthlessly exploited the most useful and indispensable section of the population only to squander the wealth so hardly produced.'

Even more distasteful for Joseph were demands that restrictions be placed on the absolute power of the emperor. Alarming evidence began to accumulate that these opinions were not confined to the men who wrote them. Radical preachers in the suburbs attracted large congregations and worried officials warned of growing discontent. Specific political grievances were given extra momentum by the economic crisis of the late 1780s. In part this was due to a general European depression but to Joseph's subjects it seemed that his misguided economic policy and in particular his war against the Turks were responsible. Increased taxation to pay for the war, the new conscription system to provide the men and high food prices created an ugly mood. In the summer of 1788 bread riots broke out in Vienna. Referring to the French Revolution, Caroline Pichler wrote in her memoirs: 'Here too in Austria these violent tremors made themselves felt. There was much secret muttering and smouldering and everywhere there was loud expression of opposition, discontent with the existing situation and increasingly severe criticism of the actions and orders of the monarch.' (**10**).

Afraid that the beast he had released might turn on its liberator, Joseph made strenuous efforts to regain control. His chosen instrument to prevent popular enlightenment from becoming popular revolution was the reorganised police force (**111**). Under the direction of the Minister of the Interior Count Pergen, a network of agents was spread across the Monarchy. Originally they were intended to be welfare workers as well as law enforcement officers but, as fears of insurrection grew, this former function receded into the background. They were ordered to maintain an unceasing vigil over the subjects in their district and to report the slightest hint of a disturbance. An invidious system of informers was set up, by which rewards were promised to private citizens who reported the misdemeanours of their neighbours. In his enthusiasm to extinguish even the smallest sparks of rebellion, Joseph contravened frequently the rule of law which earlier he had advocated so fervently (**104**). The regular judicial procedure was bypassed, subjects were held in custody without trial and *agents provocateurs* were used to obtain evidence to convict. At the same time steps were taken to restrict and decelerate the spread of the Enlightenment. Individual professors were ordered to moderate the public expression of their views and a review of all the educational reforms was begun. Finally, strict censorship regulations were reimposed, for—as Joseph wrote one month before his death—'It is generally recognised that books, the contents of which are calculated to undermine the principles of all religion, morality and social care, to promote the disintegration of all ties uniting states and nations, are in fact dangerous in their effects and it is therefore a duty towards humanity to prevent, as far as possible, the circulation of such books.'

In this partial retreat from his enlightened despotism Joseph was seen at his worst. The dubious tactics he employed to stifle political dissent were contrary to everything taught by enlightened jurists. Nor were they necessary. The repression owed more to Joseph's uncompromising character than to the facts of the situation. Despite all the attention lavished on his political opponents, there was never any danger that a full-scale revolution of the French variety would erupt in the Habsburg Monarchy. Outside Vienna the radicals were of negligible importance, if indeed they existed at all, while among the quarter of a million inhabitants of the capital they could be counted only in hundreds. The importance attached to the Austrian revolutionaries was based largely on the imaginative reports o f Count Pergen's agents (**102**). What is often forgotten is that spies are paid on results and that if they cannot find a real conspiracy they will be sorely tempted to invent one. The 'Jacobin Plot' which was uncovered in 1794, after Joseph's death, was composed of a motley collection of idealists, adventurers and *agents provocateurs;* only eight were sent to the gallows, six of them in Hungary. The social and economic structure of Vienna made the city curiously resistant to revolution. Although there were some large commercial and industrial enterprises there, it was first and foremost a residential city [**doc. 16**]. As one contemporary, Friedrich Nicolai, observed: 'Austria has more princes and counts as great vassals than any other German state; and almost all of them spend most of the year in Vienna. Part of the great vassals of Bohemia and especially of Hungary prefer to consume their large incomes in Vienna than on their estates' (**8**). These nobles were the mainstay of the city's economy. Without them the luxury and service industries would collapse overnight, without them the thousands of domestic servants would be thrown out of work. The enormous amount of money put into circulation by the nobility dictated not only the economic structure of the city, but also made it prosperous. J. C. Riesbeck wrote: 'The number of poor is much smaller than at Paris, and, probably, than at London. Everything, even the clothing of the lowest servant-maid, bespeaks a great degree of affluence' (**11**). In this aristocratic atmosphere egalitarian ideas fell upon stony ground. It is not surprising that the mastercraftsmen, or the journeymen and apprentices who aspired to succeed them, proved unreceptive to suggestions that their best customers be ejected. The Enlightenment had made few converts among the ordinary citizens, as was shown by their attachment to the old forms of worship. The main protagonists of the Austrian Enlightenment were academics and officials. They were committed to all manner of reforms but, as state employees, were naturally opposed to revolution. There was no group of intellectuals independent of and opposed to the establishment which could be compared with the philosophes in France. As was mentioned above, Caroline Pichler believed that a revolutionary mood did prevail in Vienna at the end of the 1780s but others, such as Joseph Pezzl, saw only somnolent conservatism. Both assessments were probably exaggerated. There was certainly some discontent and in the bad winter of 1788/9 there was some hardship but the situation was in no way comparable to that in France. One bread riot does not make a revolution.

If Vienna could not provide the revolutionary initiative, then it was even less likely to come from the rest of the Monarchy. Joseph's main problem was not the radicalism of his subjects but their incorrigible conservatism. In the rural areas, where illiteracy was the norm and where rights were understood in terms of grazing on

D

common lands, the Roman Catholic Church was a massive bastion of stability. It might incite the peasants to resist Joseph's religious reforms but it would never send them marching to Vienna in the name of liberty and equality. The peasants' position was always miserable and often intolerable, but they lacked the ability to organise themselves on a national scale. Even had it been possible it would have been futile to have launched an insurrection against an emperor who represented their only chance of emancipation. An isolated jacquerie against an individual landlord was no danger to the state. It was ironic that the provincialism which had foiled Joseph's reforms should ensure stability in an age of revolution. 'The nation' and 'national sovereignty' were alien concepts in a Monarchy which was still only the sum total of its component provinces. The revolution in Belgium did not provoke a sympathetic spasm in Carinthia and if the Hungarians had raised the standard of revolt the Tyroleans would not have rallied to it. Appreciating this, an Austrian official argued against too much uniformity, because 'the quick success of the revolution in France had been due to the uniformity of the population' (**104**). The very weakness of the Monarchy bred a natural resistance to radical innovations, whether they came from above or below.

It is possible, although it cannot be established, that the French Revolution made some of Joseph's literate subjects more aware of their political tutelage but there is no real point of comparison between the Habsburg Monarchy and France in 1789. The malcontents borrowed the language of the French revolutionaries but their aims were entirely different. An historian of Hungary has written in a recent article: 'The concept [The Social Contract] owed nothing to Rousseau but its name. It was limited only to the rights of the nobility and served as a slogan for these gentlemen in their fight for their own particularistic interests,' and 'the Hungarian burgher did not have the power of the French bourgeois; only a strong king, like Joseph II, could win for him his battle with the nobility. So the burghers, like the nobles, adapted French ideas to their own aims and used them to demand not only the abolition of the nobility but also a return to absolute monarchy' (**105**). The approval which some intellectuals bestowed on the French Revolution must not be interpreted as a desire for a revolution in their own country. Pietro Verri, who resigned his post in Milan in protest at Joseph's authoritarian government, wrote to his brother: 'We are faithful to our sovereign. . . . We pray to God to keep far from us the turbulent movements which convulse all Europe' (**93**).

When Joseph died the only mourners were the peasants and some Josephist officials and academics. Some of his projects had been failures, some had been foolish and many had been unpopular. Yet the system as a whole had not been brought into disrepute. His subjects may have resented his ecclesiastical innovations or foreign adventures but at the same time his egalitarianism and his social welfare policies convinced them that he had their interests at heart. It was easy to hate Joseph but difficult to despise him. The reign was a fine illustration of one of Goethe's rare but perceptive political maxims: 'Hate destroys no one, it is contempt that drags men down'. Goethe was thinking of the likeable but pathetic Louis XVI and the comparison is revealing. It was never remotely possible that the detestable but iron-willed Joseph would end his days on the guillotine.

Joseph died in his bed at the age of forty-nine. The problems he had wrestled with had engaged, absorbed, and then exhausted even his phenomenal energies. In time provincial loyalties might have softened, a new bureaucracy might have been created and the next generation might have emerged enlightened from the new schools but time could not be directed by an exercise of will.

Part Three

CONCLUSION

6 Joseph II and the Enlightened Despots

The unique quality of Joseph's achievement, the problems he faced and the degree of his failure are thrown into sharper relief by a comparison with the other contemporary rulers usually bracketed together under the heading 'enlightened despots'. The two who most commonly are put into harness with Joseph are Frederick the Great and Catherine the Great, who owe their position more to the size and importance of their territories than to the Enlightenment which they preached and practised. There were some striking similarities between the policies of the three rulers, some minor differences and one difference of major importance.

Although Joseph fought a running battle with Frederick in the field of international relations, he had only the greatest respect for him as a man and political reformer. In view of Joseph's customary inability to approve of anyone but himself, his description of Frederick as a 'genius' was praise indeed. It is probable that Frederick had considerable influence on the formation of Joseph's political creed, for he was the first European absolute monarch to publicise his belief in the contractual theory of the state. Frederick held that once civil society had been formed it was essential for one man to assume absolute power but he insisted that the ruler was bound to observe the terms of the contract. He was not above the state but was its first servant. In the political testament of 1752 Frederick wrote: 'It is the first duty of the citizen to serve his country; it is an obligation which I have attempted to fulfil during all the various stages of my life. Charged as I am with the first magistracy, I have had the opportunity and the means of making myself useful to my fellow-citizens' (**152**). Consequently, the activities of the ruler were restricted and determined by the interests of the individuals who composed the state. He was obliged to establish and observe a rule of law, administer the economy in the interests of the whole and allow freedom of conscience. Frederick envisaged the state as a giant cooperative enterprise, in which idleness was tolerated only in the lunatic, the disabled and the old. These views were in marked contrast to those of his Hohenzollern predecessors. They had based their authority on divine right and had regarded their scattered territories as their personal property. Typical of their patrimonial attitude was Frederick William I's blunt claim: 'We are Lord and Master and can do what we like' (**153**). They behaved responsibly towards their subjects because they feared the wrath of their Calvinist God and because of their loyalty to the Hohenzollern family. They wished to hand on to their sons a piece of property which was better organised and more productive than that which they themselves had inherited. Frederick abolished the dichotomy between ruler and subject (or 'property') and made political obligation dependent on purely secular considerations.

Frederick and Joseph shared the same fundamental assumptions about the object of political activity and deduced from them similar practical measures for the ruler to implement. Frederick's major achievement in the domestic sphere was his establishment of the rule of law (**145**). On his accession the administration of justice in Prussia was as complex as the assorted parcels of territory which made up the Hohenzollern inheritance. Military, political, administrative and fiscal unity had been imposed on this conglomeration by 1740 but justice had been neglected. To assist them in their task of raising and paying for an enormous army, the various Prussian administrative bodies had been equipped with judicial powers. In any matter affecting the royal domains or the revenues of the state the provincial authorities were empowered to prosecute individual subjects. This may have made for greater administrative efficiency but it was clearly not in the interests of justice that an individual subject could be confronted by the local official acting as both accuser and judge. In addition, the development of 'administrative justice' confused further the already nebulous demarcation lines which defined the competence of the various judicial bodies. The introduction of order into the chaotic situation was supervised by Samuel von Cocceji but it was his master Frederick who laid down the principles and who supported him when the Prussian vested interests called for his dismissal. Under Cocceji and his successors Jariges, Carmer and Suarez a single coherent system was established, from which a litigant could obtain a judgment quickly and cheaply. The administrative bodies were not stripped completely of their judicial powers but the latter were restricted severely. Substance was not given to the reformed structure until after Frederick's death but, although posthumous, the General Code (*Allgemeines Landrecht*) of 1794 was an achievement of Frederick's reign. It remained in force in Prussia until 1900. Like Joseph, Frederick also attempted to introduce humanity into the Criminal Code. He abolished torture and the use of mutilation and executions as punishments for trivial offences. Anglo-Saxon historians have failed to attach sufficient importance to these 'legal reforms'. In the absence of a representative constitution of the kind to be found in the United States or Great Britain, the laws and the way in which they were administered represented the subject's only protection against arbitrary oppression. In the political testament of 1752 Frederick wrote: 'I have decided never to intervene in the course of justice; for in the courts only the laws should speak and the ruler should remain silent', and he laid even greater emphasis on this principle in the testament of 1768: 'The ruler may never intervene in the course of justice. The laws alone should rule. The duty of the ruler is restricted to protecting them' (**152**). Frederick remained loyal to his principles but there was no constitutional guarantee that his successors would be equally enlightened. In theory Joseph II also subscribed to the doctrine of non-interference, but at the end of his reign, when there were fears of a revolution, he found the temptation to make use of his absolute power irresistible.

Frederick differed sharply from Joseph on the question of religion. The latter was a devout Catholic, albeit of a somewhat unorthodox kind; Frederick despised all revealed religion. He referred to Christianity as 'an old metaphysical fiction, full of the supernatural, contradictions and absurdities, born in the passionate imagination of the Orientals.' Both men agreed however that reason, humanity and the Social Contract demanded religious toleration. Frederick summed up his religious policy with the celebrated words 'I am neutral between Rome and Geneva'. He allowed sects such as the Hussites and the Anti-Trinitarians, which could find refuge nowhere else in Europe, to settle in Prussia, to build churches and to practise their particular 'metaphysical fiction' freely. He proclaimed that he would welcome Muslims and build them mosques if they could show that they would be useful to the state. Perhaps his most flamboyant gesture of toleration was to build for the Roman Catholics of Berlin a magnificent church next door to the royal palace. Previous Hohenzollern kings had practised toleration in the interests of economic expansion but Frederick's policy was more systematic and based on more than material considerations. (**145**)

Frederick's economic policies were rigidly mercantilist (**129**). His state monopolies, state-sponsored trading companies and protectionist tariffs were all reminiscent of those of his great-grandfather, Frederick William the Great Elector. These policies may have been the only way to promote economic expansion in 'the sand-box of Europe' but they certainly owed nothing to contemporary economic theories. Prussia during his reign was a physiocrat's nightmare. Like Joseph, he sought to reform the guilds but never contemplated anything as radical as a uniform land tax. He sought to make the existing economic system more productive, and in this he enjoyed considerable success, but he did not attempt to change it. In his attention to the material welfare of his subjects, however, he betrayed the influence of the Enlightenment and anticipated Joseph's reforms of the 1780s. By 1768 he could write in the second political testament that Prussia did not lack institutions for the old, the lunatic, the sick, the poor, orphans and widows. By his erection of state granaries and control of the grain trade he succeeded in maintaining the price of bread at a reasonable level in the frequent years of scarcity. Many contemporaries would have agreed with the English diplomat who commented that he would rather be 'a monkey in Borneo' than a subject of the King of Prussia but conditions were more tolerable in 1786 than in 1740.

Frederick's domestic legislation is often dismissed as traditional Hohenzollernism writ large. The continuity of the period 1640 to 1786 is certainly striking, particularly with respect to administration and social structure. Nevertheless, his establishment of a rule of law, extension of religious toleration and policies of social welfare indicated that he was influenced by the political philosophy of the Enlightenment. Parallels can be drawn between Prussia and Austria during this period not only from coincidence or from the international situation demanding an increase in the power of the state but also because Frederick II and Joseph II shared a common political outlook. This is much less clear in the case of Russia. Histories of Catherine the Great are legion, but as they usually concentrate either on her sexual excesses or on the enlightened and 'western European' aspects of her policy, there is good reason to discuss at some length the other side of her reign. Catherine's place in the ranks of the enlightened despots is a result not so much of what she did as of what she said and, more important, of what contemporaries said about her. Until the French Revolution reminded her of the dangers of even boudoir enlightenment, Catherine conducted a voluminous correspondence with the literary giants of western Europe. The relationship remained platonic, the only issue being *billets-doux*, but her passion did not go unrequited. Grimm told her that he cried like a calf when he received her letters and his French colleagues vied with each other in the composition of absurd flatteries. The affair showed the philosophes at their worst. Conveniently isolated from real conditions in Russia, they chose to believe everything that Catherine told them and ignored all evidence to the contrary (**26**). In any assessment of her relationship with the Enlightenment, the hyperbole of the philosophes is as irrelevant as, in the case of Frederick the Great, the fact that he played the flute and wrote bad French poetry.

Apart from this plethora of mutual admiration, Catherine's reputation rests on her Instruction of 1767 and the Legislative Commission summoned to discuss it. Clear evidence of her enthusiasm for and knowledge of the Enlightenment was provided by the wholesale plagiarism she indulged in. Of the 655 paragraphs of the Instruction, 250 were borrowed directly from Montesquieu and 100 from Beccaria. That coherent thought of any kind should emanate from Russia was startling enough, that it should bear strong signs of enlightened influence sent the philosophes into a veritable ecstasy of delight. Voltaire compared her favourably with Lycurgus and Solon and proclaimed the Instruction to be 'the most beautiful monument of the century'. The Legislative Commission however proved unable and unwilling to translate the good intentions of the empress into action. When the delegates dispersed at the end of 1768 they had nothing to show for eighteen months of talk. The official reason for the closure was the Turkish War, which required the return of noble and Cossack deputies to their regiments. This is unacceptable, for the Commission had been run down long before the war broke out in October, 1768 (**115**). Nor can its failure be attributed solely to the inexperience and illiteracy of its members. The Commission floundered in a procedural mire, which Catherine had created and which she did nothing to alter when the plight of the delegates became apparent. Everything was read, there was no spontaneous debate. A great deal of time was wasted in reading extracts from the Instruction, the *cahiers* of the delegates and old laws. A deputy wishing to make a proposal read a written speech to the plenary assembly. Those of his colleagues who agreed with the opinions expressed, signed their names at the bottom of the document. This did not constitute a formal vote, deputies in opposition could obtain a postponement to allow them to draw up counterproposals. This procedure could of course be extended indefinitely. On 12 October 1767, for example, an opinion was read on peasants engaging in trade; a reply followed on 24 October, another on 2 November, yet another on 12 November, and so on. Recent research has suggested strongly, if it has not proved, that there was no causal relationship between the Instruction and the Commission. Catherine began work on the former in 1763 but there was no mention of the Commission until May 1766. The clauses in the Instruction which made it seem that she had always intended to summon a representative assembly were inserted later. The attractive picture of a liberal empress summoning representatives of her subjects to discuss reforms and composing an enlightened treatise to guide their deliberations must be abandoned.

As the Instruction cost Catherine a great deal of time and the Commission cost her a great deal of money, it is clear that she thought that the project would prove to be worth while. Later in her reign Catherine claimed that the Commission had provided her with a great deal of useful information about her empire but this was retrospective justification rather than an indication of her original motives. Doubtless the applause of the philosophes rang sweet in her ears but it is doubtful whether even Catherine's vanity could demand a public relations exercise of this scale. The real explanation of the summoning of the Commission lay in the way in which Catherine came to power and in the insecurity of the first few years of her reign. In June and July 1762 her deranged and hated husband, Peter III, was deposed and then murdered by a group of guards led by Catherine's current lover, Gregor Orlov. Many of the nobles who had assisted or connived at the *coup d'état* thought only in terms of the new empress being regent, until her son Paul came of age. Catherine had other ideas of course but she was aware that having risen by the sword she ran the risk of perishing by the sword. The Prussian ambassador echoed the views of many contemporaries when he wrote to Frederick: 'It is certain that the reign of the Empress Catherine is not to be more than a brief episode in the history of the world.' It is probable that d'Alembert's refusal of her invitation to go to Russia to act as a tutor for Paul was based on fears for her position. In 1766 rumours spread in western Europe that she had been poisoned in a counter-*coup*. However false, these predictions of her imminent downfall were not just wishful thinking. Inevitably Catherine had been unable to reward all her fellow-conspirators in accordance with their wishes; they resented particularly the favouritism shown towards the Orlov brothers. In 1764 a group of disaffected army officers nearly succeeded in freeing the ex-Tsar Ivan VI, who had been deposed in 1741 and had been in prison ever since. A rash of pretenders appeared, men claiming to be Peter III, Ivan VI and a son of George II of England and the Tsarina Elisabeth. In 1765 an insurrection broke out led by a man claiming to be Peter the Great, who had been dead forty years. Some of these plots were of negligible importance but they were a constant reminder to Catherine of the instability of her position.

The Legislative Commission was designed to strengthen the foundations of her rule (**115**). It was certainly not intended to be a vehicle for greater participation by the Russian people in affairs of state. The passages in the Instruction relating to the power of the monarch were quite uncompromising: 'The sovereign is absolute. The extent of the empire necessitates absolute power in the ruler. Any other form of government would have ruined it.' Catherine borrowed a great deal of Montesquieu's judicial theory but nothing of his political theory; there was no mention of the *pouvoirs intermédiaires* on which he had laid great stress. Absolutism demanded independence from the magnates who had brought her to power and it was this which the Commission was designed to achieve. In contrast to the previous commissions, the noble delegates were in a minority. The administration sent 27 delegates, the nobles 160, the towns 200, the free peasants 50, the Inorodzy or 'foreign people' 50, and the population of the military frontier regions 70. The predominance of the non-noble element was achieved by the deliberate manipulation of the electoral laws. Prince Shcherbatov, the most prominent and articulate of the noble deputies, wrote:

As it seems to me, the number of gentlemen deputies of other ranks apart from the nobility is larger than the number of noble deputies. So it will not be the corps of the nobility, the most enlightened about the true advantages of the fatherland, who will decide, so much as, because of the preponderance of their number, the merchants, heathen tribes, state peasants, and similar people, who for the most part have never been honoured with such a great task, and are without an understanding of each aspect of the general situation of the Empire (**125**).

By bringing the backwoods gentry to Moscow she reminded the magnates of the traditional alliance between Tsars and lesser nobility. By confronting the nobility as a class with a large number of deputies from other sections of society, she attached the latter more firmly to her person and demonstrated to the former that they were not the only force in Russian society. By simply calling the Commission and having its members solemnly recognise her on the throne, she legitimised the *coup d'état* of 1762 and reduced her dependence on those who had brought her to power. Before 1767 she did not dare to decide on any matter personally. One special commission after another was created to discuss and advise on such matters as the rights of the nobility, the secularisation of church land and commerce. After 1768 these commissions and with them any participation by the nobility in policy-making disappeared. Catherine had established herself in fact as well as in theory as an absolute monarch. When the Commission had fulfilled its task, she discarded it, using the Turkish War as a convenient pretext. Better informed and less naïve than Catherine's sycophantic coterie of French admirers, the foreign diplomats in Russia were under no illusions as to the real purpose of the Commission. The British ambassador reported that: 'By these and other similar measures, glittering enough to dazzle the eyes of the Russians, the power of Her Imperial Majesty increases every day, and is already arrived to such a degree that this prudent princess thinks herself strong enough to humble the guards, who placed her upon the throne.'

It is probable that the information Catherine acquired in the course of the Commission's 'deliberations' served as a basis for her later legislation. What is questionable is whether the principles enunciated in the Instruction exercised any influence. In only two spheres are traces of the Enlightenment discernible. Her ecclesiastical policy was certainly similar to that of Joseph and Frederick, in its extension of the control of the state. No papal bulls could be admitted without the government's consent and the secularisation of church land, begun by Peter III, continued apace. Toleration was granted to the Mohammedans and the many bizarre sects of the

South. Also reminiscent of Josephist policy were the restrictions imposed on the monasteries: the minimum age for the profession of vows was raised, and the founding of new religious houses was forbidden. Catherine also displayed considerable interest in popular education. The Statute of Popular Schools of 1782 was the work of the Serb Iankovitch, a graduate of the University of Vienna who had been sent to Russia by Joseph II at Catherine's request. By her death 508 schools with an attendance of 22,210 had been founded. Although this represented very considerable progress in relative terms, only a tiny minority of the population was affected. Apart from the new creations there were only 549 educational establishments of any kind in Russia, with a total attendance of 61,966. In the words of an historian who is more willing than most to see the bright side of Catherine's reign: 'The vast majority of the Russian people of all classes at this time were little affected by the new forces of enlightenment, but still finding their ideas and their faith where their ancestors had found them' (**125**).

For all her fine words in the Instruction about the duties incumbent on a ruler, Catherine's attention to the welfare of her subjects left a great deal to be desired. She was a woman of immense vanity, was highly susceptible to flattery, liked to believe that all was for the best in the best of all possible Russias and was out of touch with real conditions in her Empire. In 1781 a truly absurd report was presented to her which reviewed numerically the achievements of the first nineteen years of her reign: 29 provincial administrations had been reorganised according to the new system, 144 towns had been built, 30 treaties or conventions had been signed, 78 victories had been won, 88 edicts relating to laws and institutions and 123 to lighten the burden on the people had been promulgated. This came to a grand total of 492 beneficent actions. This document was sent to Baron von Grimm for his adulation, complete with a smirking letter from the empress (**115**). As her servants knouted, pillaged and raped their way through the provinces, she wrote to her French friends that nowhere in Europe could such dedicated and talented officials be found as in Russia. The non-Russian minorities in the frontier regions suffered particularly. One official called out the military to assist him in cattle-rustling, and in October 1770 75,000 caravans fled across the southern frontiers to seek refuge from the exactions of Catherine's dedicated and talented administration. The officials were of course only too happy to foster the myth. On the

occasion of her journey to the Crimea with Joseph II in 1787 every
effort was made to present the area to her as prosperous and happy.
Travellers reported how groups of merry singing peasants were lined
up along the banks of rivers in gaily decorated boats, how large herds
of cattle were collected and driven into prominent positions and how
markets stocked with all kinds of goods were set up. Needless to
say, the latter were not permanent fixtures. The orders of the
provincial government of Charkov as to how the people were to
behave still survive: they were to put on their best clothes, tramps
and drunks were to be removed, women and girls were to strew
flowers at Catherine's feet, everyone was to display their rapture in
the appropriate way, houses on the imperial route were to be freshly
painted and in a good state of repair, from all windows costly cloth
and carpets were to be hung, there was to be no begging, absolutely
no petitions were to be presented and all magistrates were to ensure
that no increase in prices coincided with the visit and that only
goods of the best quality were on display (**115**). The Prince de
Ligne reported that while stories of villages being constructed of
paper were exaggerated, it was true that Catherine never went
anywhere on foot, that the towns which looked finished had no
streets, the streets no houses and the houses no windows, roofs or
doors. The duplicity of her officials and the primitive nature of
Russian communications were partly responsible for the confine-
ment of Catherine to a gilded cage but one suspects that it also
suited her inclinations.

Catherine's casual disregard of the interests of her subjects was
also apparent in her attitude to finance. Expenditure rose by almost
500 per cent during the reign but income failed to keep pace. The
ever-increasing deficit was met by loans and in particular by the
issue of paper money. The immediate effect of this latter expedient
was inflation and a steep rise in the cost of living. The details of this
massive expenditure are most instructive: 37 per cent went to the
army and navy, 13·5 per cent to the court and less than 1·5 per cent
to education and welfare (**125**). As the figures for the court indicated, Catherine was incorrigibly extravagant. Even western
European travellers, accustomed to displays of opulence by their
own princes, were astounded by the sybaritic luxury of her court.
The celebrated journey to the Crimea was scheduled to cost 10
million roubles, or about 12·5 per cent of the total annual budget,
but in the event much more was needed. Catherine was particularly

generous to her lovers, even after they had been retired from their stud duties. Potemkin was placed in charge of the newly conquered territories in the south and was given full power and a great deal of money to indulge his fevered imagination. The showpiece of his grandiose scheme was to be a new town on the river Dnieper: Jekaterinoslav. Typical of the scale and fatuity of the project was the cathedral. Potemkin insisted that it be two feet longer than St Peter's at Rome, so that it would be the largest church in the world. Predictably, the whole scheme was a gigantic and costly failure. In 1787 Catherine and Joseph II arrived to lay the foundation stones. With an uncharacteristic flash of wit Joseph commented that on that day they had achieved a singular feat: Catherine had laid the first stone of a city and he had laid the last (**100**). He was almost right. Of the few buildings actually completed, the most prominent was a magnificent palace for Potemkin.

Catherine's irresponsible attitude to the administration of her country was in marked contrast to that of Frederick the Great and Joseph II. The latter pair's domestic programme indicated that they took seriously the implications of the social contract. All sorts of qualifications have to be made of course about the actual implementation of their good intentions. The shortcomings of Joseph's bureaucracy and the reluctance of the officials to enforce the emperor's ordinances have already been discussed. The same sort of criticisms can also be levelled at the Prussian system. Frederick, whose arsenal of abusive epithets rivalled that of Joseph, referred to some of his officials as 'vile human trash who steal like magpies'. Despite a sustained barrage of criticism and threats from their king, the Prussian bureaucrats provided yet another example of the peculiar ability of civil servants to observe no rules but their own. Frederick tried hard but abuses such as nepotism, social discrimination and inter- and intra-departmental disputes were never eradicated. Acutely conscious of their elite status, the noble officials combined and conspired to obstruct measures which eroded their position (**147**). Nevertheless, in relative terms, the Prussian administration was conspicuously more loyal and honest than its counterparts in other European states in the same period. Referring to the reign of Frederick the Great, Gerhard Ritter wrote: 'Military discipline and promptness, competence and complete integrity were the glories of the old Prussian bureaucracy' (**145**). Nebulous though it may sound, the *style* of Joseph's and Frederick's government was very different from that of Catherine. For all their idiosyncrasies, Prussia and Austria were recognisably European in the 1780s. The same cannot be said of Russia.

Similarities between either or both of the two monarchs of eastern Europe and Joseph II pale into insignificance when compared with their divergent attitude towards the nobility and serfdom. The thinkers of the Enlightenment were opposed to both institutions on grounds of reason, humanity and economic efficiency. His establishment of a unitary state, abolition of personal serfdom and tax decree of 1789 showed that Joseph agreed with them. It is impossible to imagine him applauding the views of Frederick the Great, as expressed in his Political Testament of 1752: 'A sovereign ought to regard it as his duty to protect the nobility, which forms the most beautiful jewel in his crown and the lustre of his army . . . it is the duty of the state to preserve the nobility because whereas other classes may surpass them in wealth, none surpasses them in valour or fidelity' (**152**). In this respect Frederick was more conservative than his predecessors. The attack by the Great Elector and Frederick William I on the privileges of the estates and their employment of commoners in the administration and the army indicated that they did not share Frederick's enthusiasm for 'the most beautiful jewel' in the Prussian crown (**131**). Frederick William I had pursued a vigorous policy of reclaiming extensive parts of the royal domains which had been usurped by the nobles over the centuries. By deft use of the judicial powers of his administrative bodies he increased enormously the acreage of his domains. By 1740, however, the political power of the nobility was a thing of the past and Frederick could indulge his aristocratic prejudices without endangering his absolute power. He purged the commoners from the upper ranks of the civil service and the officer corps. He stopped the reclamation of domain land. He offered them positive assistance in the shape of subsidies for the improvement of their estates and the repair of war damage. He set up credit institutions to remedy their chronic lack of capital. Above all, he allowed them to retain their absolute power over their serfs. On the royal domains labour services were restricted to three or four days a week and hereditary tenure was granted, but elsewhere the serfs were abandoned to the tender mercies of their lords. In 1763 Frederick contemplated abolishing serfdom in Pomerania but abandoned the project in the face of opposition from the Junkers. Quite deliberately, Frederick created a state which was even more rigidly stratified than that of his predecessors. The three separate orders had three separate functions: the nobility administered and protected the state, the bourgeoisie provided the wealth, the peasants provided the raw material for the army. These functions were mutually exclusive; the nobility could not engage in trade and the bourgeoisie could not buy noble land. If by some cataclysmic display of inefficiency or extravagance a noble was compelled to sell his land, then it had to be bought by another member of his class.

Catherine's policy was very similar. The two most important pieces of domestic legislation in her reign were the administrative reorganisation of 1775 and the Nobles' Charter of 1785 (**125**). The most striking feature of the former lay less in the structural alterations it introduced than in its reinforcement of noble predominance in the localities. The nobility of the districts within the provinces received the right to elect the two district officials, whose powers included the enforcement of government ordinances, the supervision of transport, fire precautions and public health, the billeting of troops, the recapture of runaway serfs and the maintenance of public order. The nobles were also empowered to elect the subordinate officials of the law courts, while the officials in charge of the towns and the courts dealing with state and free peasants were selected by the central government from the ranks of the nobility. Their position was strengthened further by the 'Charter of the Rights, Freedoms and Privileges of the Noble Russian Dvorinastvo' of 1785. Most of the rights enumerated in the Charter had been enjoyed by the nobility for some considerable time but their codification in a document sealed with imperial approval was the consummation of noble hegemony in Russian society. The most important innovation was the provision for provincial and district assemblies. At their triennial meetings the nobles could discuss grievances and present demands to the empress through the provincial governors.

The necessary corollary of this attention to the interests of the nobility was the neglect of the serfs. In the salons of St Petersburg Russian nobles dressed in the latest Parisian fashions discussed the latest products of the French Enlightenment; they went to the theatre to see the latest French plays, they went to their art dealers to buy the latest French paintings. But Russia was more than St Petersburg. In Astrakhan, Irkutsk and Ochotsk life continued as it had done since time immemorial. Unlike Frederick of Prussia,

107

Conclusion

Catherine made frequent reference to her disapproval of serfdom but she did nothing about it. Before the Commission was summoned she gave 1,000 ducats to the Free Economic Society to be used as a prize for the best essay on emancipation. Yet the serfs were not represented at the Commission and the question of emancipation did not appear amongst its agenda. The earlier drafts of the Instruction contained paragraphs referring to the need to give the serfs greater protection against the oppression of their lords but the opposition of her councillors excised them from the final product. In the event, the question was raised at the Commission but the violent abuse exchanged between the free peasants and a few liberal nobles on one side and the bulk of the nobility on the other did nothing to help the serfs. Catherine's attitude was not only irresolute, it was also equivocal. A number of her actions were irreconcilable with her professed abhorrence of serfdom. In 1765 the lords were empowered to imprison the serfs at will, and to send them to Siberia without reference to the regular courts and without right of appeal. In 1767 they lost the right to complain to the public authorities (**121**). Despite her well-publicised interest in emancipation schemes, she made large grants of serfs with land to her favourites and imposed serfdom on the Ukraine, where it had never existed before. In the course of her reign she turned some 800,000 state peasants into privately owned serfs. In contrast to the Habsburg territories or Prussia, in Russia the serfs continued to be sold openly without land. In the Moscow newspapers they were advertised like cattle—'by the family' or 'individually', with 'attractive girl serfs' fetching particularly high prices.

Denied any constitutional means of protest, the serfs repeatedly took the law into their own hands by rising in revolt. There were always insurrections raging in Russia. They were local, uncoordinated and easily suppressed but in 1773 one of the most violent jacqueries in modern European history broke out. Led by a Cossack deserter called Pugachev, an enormous mob of serfs ravaged central and southern Russia and kept the imperial army at bay for more than a year. Pugachev's claim to be Peter III was largely irrelevant, but what did bring the serfs flocking to his standard was his declaration of war on the lords. Once the government had had time to mobilise an army of regular troops the revolt was doomed but its ferocity and duration were ample evidence of Catherine's failure to alleviate the miserable lot of the majority of her subjects. For them

108

it made little difference whether Catherine the Enlightened or Ivan the Terrible sat on the throne of Russia (**115**).

In this fundamental respect the policies of Frederick and Catherine differed sharply from those of Joseph. They invited the charge that they had ignored the enlightened principles they liked to profess but they could have argued in their own defence that they were simply facing up to the realities of the situation. They appreciated that the cooperation of the nobility was essential for the effective administration of their countries, with their predominantly agricultural economies and their sparse, scattered and illiterate populations. In the absence of an educated urban middle class, from which a professional bureaucracy could have been recruited, the nobles were indispensable. In exchange for absolute power at a national level it was necessary to hand over to them absolute power on their estates. Any attempt to alter the traditional structure of society would have led not only to administrative inefficiency but also to a noble insurrection. The sacrifice of the interests of the serf on the altar of administrative necessity was distasteful but necessary. Joseph's refusal to compromise with anything of which he disapproved made him blind to these considerations. He antagonised the traditional props of the Monarchy but found nothing to put in their place. The shortcomings of his administration, the passive resistance of all his provinces, the narrowly averted revolt in Hungary and the open revolt in Belgium were persuasive arguments for compromise. This does not make Frederick's and Catherine's neglect of the serfs any more admirable, it serves merely as an explanation. 'Tout comprendre, c'est tout pardonner' is as fallacious in this context as in any other.

The alliance between monarch and noble was dictated not only by domestic considerations. Both Catherine and Frederick were as obsessed with foreign affairs as was Joseph. Between 1768 and 1774 and again between 1787 and 1792 Catherine was at war with the Turks, while Frederick's military exploits are too well known to need repeating. Both received the appellation 'the Great' not for any Enlightenment they may have preached or practised but for the large acquisitions of territory their campaigns secured for their countries. The decay of Poland and the Ottoman Empire gave all three rulers the opportunity for expansion. Their joint spoliation of the former in the First Partition of 1772 was the clearest indication that enlightened despotism was for domestic consumption only. In the field of foreign affairs Catherine and Frederick were very much more successful than Joseph. This was due partly to their superior military and diplomatic skills but also to their sense of priorities. They appreciated that aggression abroad and radical reform at home were incompatible. Just as they depended on the nobles to administer their countries, so they depended on the nobles to fight their wars. The idea of an army officered by commoners simply did not occur to them. In return for their services, the nobles were allowed to retain their dominant position in society. Moreover, any attack on noble privileges raised the spectre of revolution. A peasant jacquerie, even as violent as that of Pugachev, was of necessity an ephemeral embarrassment but a rebellion led by nobles was quite a different matter. Russian history in particular was punctuated frequently by palace revolutions, *coups d'état* and assassinations. Wisely perhaps, Catherine and Frederick never put the loyalty of their nobles to the test. As was stressed in an earlier chapter, there was no necessary conflict between *raison d'état* and the Enlightenment but an ambitious foreign policy could lead to tension. If a conflict did arise then both Frederick and Catherine had no hesitation in turning a deaf ear to the dictates of the Enlightenment. The great Prussian historian Otto Hintze summarised Frederick's views on the subject thus: 'It is true that together with power the welfare of the country, the happiness of the subjects, appears as an object of governmental activity but welfare is not a supreme object of equal status with power . . . the attempt to promote welfare must be adapted harmoniously to the organisation of power; they can be pursued only in so far as this harmony allows' (**131**). Joseph refused to admit that a conflict could arise. His uncompromising character demanded that he should pursue both, simultaneously, with equal vigour and ultimately to the detriment of both. Consequently he was both more ambitious and a bigger failure than his counterparts in Prussia and Russia.

In terms of simple similarity the most striking parallel was that between the legislation of Joseph and the legislation of some of the smaller European states. Many of the problems which confronted Joseph were shared with other princes and, given the international currency of enlightened ideas, it was not surprising that in many cases they adopted the same solutions. Thus the attack on ecclesiastical privileges by Charles III of Spain or by Pombal in Portugal was very reminiscent of the Josephist programme (**130**).

The dissemination of a regime's influence does not lend itself to quantitative analysis but it is clear that the influence of the Josephist model has been underestimated. It is indisputable that the theory and practice of Frederick the Great were of decisive importance in the evolution of enlightened despotism but concentration on Prussia often leads to distortion. To the many Catholic princes of the Holy Roman Empire Frederick was anathema. An atheist king of a protestant *parvenu* state (Prussia), he had disrupted the peace of Germany and by means of a treacherous attack on a defenceless young woman (Maria Theresa) he had looted an empire with which most of the Catholic princes had been allied for centuries. They were susceptible to Josephist influence not simply because the emperor was a Habsburg and a Catholic but also because their problems were so similar. In particular the problem of the Church was as acute in the Electorate of Cologne or Bavaria as it was in the Habsburg Monarchy.

The almost immediate repetition in the German principalities of measures first attempted by Joseph cannot be dismissed as coincidence. In the course of the 1780s, the Archbishop-Elector of Mainz, for example, abolished the remnants of serfdom, reformed the guilds, secularised education, dissolved monasteries, introduced a new liturgy and promoted schemes of social welfare. Many princes and intellectuals were alarmed by Joseph's aggressive foreign policy but his domestic legislation excited only their admiration. Johann Friedrich Pfeiffer, a prominent cameralist, wrote: 'The age in which we live opens up for us the most felicitous prospects; and if I ever wanted to enter the world's arena again, it would be to admire the happy results of the governmental measures, which are beyond praise, of our great Joseph II, this incomparable model of a monarch.' The German princes could afford to import the Josephist programme *en bloc* because they were not faced with the problem of the power–welfare dichotomy. Whether they liked it or not, the miniature scale of their states made an expansionist foreign policy impossible. Overshadowed by Prussia, Russia, Austria and France, they were able to attend to their domestic policies unimpeded by the demands of foreign aggression. The neglect of the lesser German principalities in favour of Prussia, which is at least understandable in the light of subsequent German history, has led to a corresponding underestimate of the international importance of Josephism. Yet the enlightened policies the princelings copied from the Austrian

111

original were largely responsible for the surprising resilience of the old regime in Germany, for the apathetic response of the masses to the French Revolution and for the stunted growth of German liberalism.

Comparisons of Joseph II with Frederick the Great or Catherine the Great are illuminating, similarities between Joseph II and numerous lesser European rulers are striking, but for his empire much more important was his relationship with his brother and successor (**110**). Leopold was called to Vienna in 1790, at a time when chaos threatened to engulf the entire Habsburg Monarchy. It was his attitude which proved decisive in determining which parts of the Josephist programme were to survive their creator. Although he hated his brother with peculiar intensity, Leopold's intellectual background and predilections were very similar. He too had been educated by Karl Anton von Martini and through him had become acquainted with the works of the philosophes. Pecuniary evidence of his enthusiasm for the Enlightenment was his subsidising of an expensive Italian edition of Diderot and D'Alembert's *Encyclopédie*. Although he was only nineteen when he went to Tuscany to rule as Grand Duke in 1765, he already possessed both a programme of reform and the determination to implement it. In view of his inexperience he was fortunate to find there a group of talented officials whose political outlook coincided with his own. Pompeo Neri, Angelo Tavanti, Gian Francesco Pagnini and Francesco Maria Gianni were all committed supporters of the Enlightenment and were all to provide him with invaluable advice and assistance during his reign of twenty-five years. Together they introduced a programme of reform which bore a close resemblance to that of Joseph. Administrative reorganisation and an attack on regional, institutional and social privileges formed a familiar background to Leopold's attempt to rejuvenate his state.

As the Tuscan Church was even more powerful than the Austrian, it was not surprising that the reformers were preoccupied with ecclesiastical affairs. The *Punti ecclesiastici*, compiled for the guidance of the diocesan synods convened in 1785, showed that Leopold had embraced the whole Jansenist programme. Dissolutions of monasteries, restrictions on those which survived, severe amortisation laws, the exclusion of papal jurisdiction, the abolition of lay brotherhoods and alterations in the liturgy were further evidence of the pervasive influence of the Josephist model. The Synod of Pistoia, which met under the auspices of its radical bishop Scipione de' Ricci in 1786, was the highwater mark of the reforms. Subsequently, opposition from conservative bishops supported by the pious population forced Leopold to adopt a more cautious attitude. In other spheres he found the vested interests less formidable and the enlightened programme was imposed without qualifications. Education was remodelled in accordance with contemporary pedagogic theory, both civil and criminal law were reformed in the spirit of Beccaria and extensive welfare schemes were introduced for the benefit of the various deprived sections of society.

Early in his reign Leopold had attracted the approving attention of the physiocrats and there is some evidence that this admiration was mutual. His removal of all restrictions on the grain trade, his reform of the guilds and his abolition of monopolies and internal customs barriers were all consonant with the physiocratic programme. Like his brother, however, Leopold was no doctrinaire disciple and was always prepared to abandon free trade when he thought it necessary, as for example when he imposed high tariffs to protect nascent Tuscan industries. As Leopold had no need to maintain a large standing army, the restrictions on his domestic legislation were correspondingly less. The influence of the Enlightenment is as striking as is the similarity with Joseph's achievement in Austria.

In one fundamental respect, however, the two brothers differed sharply. Whereas Joseph was convinced of his own infallibility and regarded all opposition as mischievous, Leopold believed that a precondition for the success of his reforms was the approval and cooperation of his subjects (**110**). He did not resent restrictions on his power, he welcomed them [**doc. 18**]. Keenly aware of the corrupting tendency of power, Leopold sought to ensure that neither he nor his successors would ever be able to govern Tuscany despotically. Before any innovation was introduced he was careful to consult with both officials and subjects. His policies were not dictated by the latter but, unlike his brother, he did believe that their legitimate interests should be taken into consideration. The most striking example of this aversion to personal absolutism was the constitutional project which engaged his attention at the beginning of the 1780s. It was no accident that he initiated discussion of the problem after a long stay in Vienna from 1778 to 1779; he had been appalled by what he called the 'despotism' of

113

Conclusion

Joseph and his chief advisers. The limitation of power had been a constant preoccupation of Leopold and in many ways the proposed constitution was the logical conclusion of his earlier administrative reforms. Although he admired the traditional estates of Belgium and Hungary, he was influenced also by modern constitutional thought and examples. There is clear evidence, for example, that he both knew and approved the terms of the constitutions of the American states. In his drafts of the new constitution he made frequent reference to Turgot, Mirabeau, Mably, d'Argenson, Martini, Rousseau, Wolff, Locke, Montesquieu, the Abbé de Saint-Pierre and many other stars of the enlightened firmament. Leopold was determined that the new representative institutions should be more than the mere decorative cyphers they had been reduced to in Austria. He was also insistent that the old tripartite division of the estates into clergy, nobility and urban commoners should be abandoned. The only division he was prepared to recognise was that between owners of real estate (*possessori*) and professional men and artisans (*artisti stabiliti*). In this respect Leopold looked forward to nineteenth-century liberalism rather than back to the medieval corporate order. Accustomed as they were to authoritarian government, enlightened or otherwise, Leopold's officials were sceptical about the project but he overrode their objections.

In September 1782 a third and final draft was completed. The written constitution reserved exclusively for the Grand Duke supreme command of the army and the power to appoint officers, ministers, bishops and officials. He also dealt directly with education. On all other matters he was obliged to consult with and obtain the approval of the representatives of his subjects. At the lowest level the latter were organised in communal assemblies, each of which selected from amongst their own number a delegate for one of the eighteen provincial assemblies, which in turn sent one delegate each to the General Assembly. This body was to meet in Florence every July. The franchise was restricted to male owners of real estate who had reached the age of twenty-five. This remarkable constitution was never introduced. The predictable opposition of the privileged classes, the political immaturity of the subjects and the unenthusiastic response of the officials were not insuperable problems. The kiss of death on the project was Joseph's plan, on the death of either him or Leopold, to abolish Tuscany's status as an independent *secundogeniture* and to reabsorb the duchy into the Habsburg Monarchy.

Tuscany was a small country, whose importance in a European context was negligible. The amount of space which has been devoted to Leopold's political views is justified by their decisive influence on the decision as to what parts of the Josephist programme were to survive in the Habsburg Monarchy as a whole. Even had there been no clamours for repeal, Leopold would have made several alterations to the system he had inherited [**doc. 18**]. His willingness to accept constitutional checks and to tolerate provincial idiosyncrasies had led him to oppose Joseph's attempt to impose absolute conformity on his various dominions. Quite deliberately he had dissociated himself from his brother's disastrous policies in Belgium and Hungary (**110**). His restoration of the old political order in these two countries and his consultation with the estates of all his dominions should be seen not as capitulation but as an extension of the system he had attempted to create in Tuscany. This diplomatic approach enabled Leopold to salvage a surprising amount of Joseph's domestic legislation from the chaos which prevailed in 1790. The general seminaries and government interference with the liturgy were abolished and a few monasteries were restored, but most of the ecclesiastical programme remained in force. Education and censorship remained in the hands of the laity and the enlightened reforms of both civil and criminal law were retained.

Had Leopold been given more time he might have developed his own distinctive political system, but he survived Joseph by only two years. In this short space he had achieved a great deal, but one recent historian's claim that the reign represented 'one step backwards, two steps forwards' is misleading (**111**). The most salient feature of Joseph's achievement had been not simply his attack on privilege but his appreciation that privileges were based on social and economic power. If he had succeeded in destroying the political, social and economic predominance of the nobles and in emancipating the peasants, he would have revolutionised his state in every sense of the word. By his abolition of the tax decree, resurrection of the estates in substantially their *old* form and restoration of the old order in Hungary Leopold ensured that noble hegemony in the Habsburg Monarchy would continue unchallenged. The peasants had to wait until 1848 for the final abolition of seignorial dues and the nobles did not lose their grip until the whole Monarchy perished at the end of the First World War. Compared with this gigantic

115

stride backwards, Leopold's forward motion was only a gentle shuffle. His son Francis II was a conservative in every respect and during his long reign the surviving sections of the Josephist structure were demolished. Joseph's influence lived on in the generation trained in his reformed universities, schools and seminaries, but the Austria which emerged in 1815 bore no relation to the dream of 1780.

All the research of recent decades has not produced a satisfactory picture of Joseph II; he remains a curiously schizophrenic character, of apparently irreconcilable contradictions. The humane egalitarian is countered by the brutal martinet, the disciple of the Enlightenment by the crude aggressor. Yet the Josephist state was unique. Although its origins were very various, the dreadful clarity of Joseph's mind, his ruthless attention to detail and his single-minded disregard of opposition gave familiar policies a character all of their own. Because the system was such a personal achievement it could only be a cul-de-sac. Quite apart from the objective reasons for its failure, it had to die with its creator. Because of its absolute nature and because Joseph's own standards were so inflexible, he must be judged a failure. For above all else, his reign had demonstrated that the complexity of human aspirations and human society will always resist attempts to impose a blueprint from above.

Part Four

DOCUMENTS

THE FUTILITY AND IRRATIONALITY OF INTOLERANCE

Although the Enlightenment was a heterogeneous movement, its adherents were unanimous on the need for toleration. Religious persecution was condemned as irrational, inhumane and prejudicial to the prosperity of the state. Voltaire's treatise was inspired by an actual case, the judicial murder of a Huguenot named Calas in Toulouse in 1763.

Natural Law is that which nature reveals to all men. . . . Human law can be founded on no other basis than the law of nature; and in every part of the globe, the great principle, the universal principle of both is 'Do nothing which you would not like done to yourself'. But in following this principle, it is impossible to see how one man can say to another 'believe that which I believe, and which you cannot believe, or you will perish'. Yet that is what is being said in Portugal, in Spain, in Goa. In some other countries at present they are content to say: 'Believe or I shall hate you; believe or I shall do you all the harm that I can; monster, if you do not share my religion, you have no religion at all: you must be cast out by your relations, your town, your province'.

If it were a human law to behave in such a fashion, it would follow necessarily that the Japanese would detest the Chinese, who in turn would loathe the Siamese; the latter would attack the Gangarides, who would descend on the inhabitants of the Indus region; a Mogol would tear out the heart of the first Malabare he met, who would slit the throat of the Persian, who would massacre the Turk: and all together they would throw themselves on the Christians, who have been engaged in slaughtering one another for so long.

The law of intolerance is, therefore, absurd and barbaric: it is the law of tigers, but more terrible still, because while tigers kill to eat, we exterminate each other for the sake of words. . . .

. . . But what! Is every citizen to be permitted to believe nothing but his reason, and to think what this enlightened or misguided reason dictates to him? Certainly he may, provided that he does not disturb the peace: for a man is not obliged to believe or not to believe, but he is obliged to observe the customs of his country; and if you say that it is a crime not to believe in the religion of the majority, then you accuse your forefathers, the early Christians, of the same offence, and you justify those who had them tortured.

You reply that there is a great difference, that all other religions are the work of men, and that only the Catholic Church, Apostolic and Roman, is the work of God. But let me seriously ask, because our religion is divine, ought it to rule by hate, by fury, by exile, by confiscation, by prison, by torture and by solemn acts of thanksgiving to the Deity for such outrages? The more the Christian religion is divine, the less it behoves man to impose it; if God created it, God will maintain it without your assistance. You know that intolerance produces only hypocrites or rebels: what miserable alternatives! Finally, do you wish to maintain by the executioner the religion of a God who perished by the executioner, and who preached only gentleness and patience?

From Voltaire: *Traité sur la Tolérance à l'occasion de la Mort de Jean Calas*, 1763, chapters vi and xi. Extracts from French and German texts have been translated by the author unless otherwise indicated.

document 2

MAXIMS OF CESARE BECCARIA

The emphasis on utility and belief in the rational nature of man prompted many attacks on the barbarities of the existing penal systems. One of the most important critics was Cesare Bonesans Marquis de Beccaria (1738–94), who held both official and academic positions in the Habsburg Duchy of Milan. The influence of his humanitarian proposals is plainly discernible in the reforms of Maria Theresa and Joseph II.

Surely the groans of the weak, sacrificed to the cruel ignorance, and indolence of the powerful; the barbarous torments lavished, and multiplied with useless severity, for crimes either not proved, or in their nature impossible; the filth and horrors of a prison, increased by the most cruel tormenter of the miserable, uncertainty, ought to have roused the attention of those whose business is to direct the opinions of mankind.

Every act of authority of one man over another, for which there is not an absolute necessity, is tyrannical.

By justice I understand nothing more than that bond which is necessary to keep the interests of individuals united; without which men would return to their original state of barbarity. All punishments which exceed the necessity of preserving this bond, are in their nature unjust.

Pleasure and pain are the only springs of action in beings endowed with sensibility.

Crimes are only to be measured by the injury done to society.

Can the groans of a tortured wretch recall the time past, or reverse the crime he has committed?

The end of punishment is, therefore, no other than to prevent the criminal from doing further injury to society, and to prevent others from committing the like offence.

All trials should be public.

Secret accusations are a manifest abuse, but consecrated by custom in many nations, where, from the weakness of the government, they are necessary. This custom makes men false and treacherous.

What a miserable government must that be, where the sovereign suspects an enemy in every subject; and, to secure the tranquillity of the public, is obliged to sacrifice the repose of every individual!

The punishment of a nobleman should in no way differ from that of the lowest member of society.

Crimes are more effectually prevented by the certainty, than the severity of punishment.

If punishments be very severe, men are naturally led to the perpetration of other crimes, to avoid the punishment due to the first.

The punishment of death is not authorised by any right.

It is a false idea of utility, that would give to a multitude of sensible beings, that symmetry and order, which inanimate matter is alone capable of receiving.

It is a false idea of utility, which, sacrificing things to names, separates the public good from that of individuals.

It is better to prevent crimes, than to punish them. This is the fundamental principle of good legislation, which is the art of conducting men to the maximum of happiness and to the minimum of misery.

Would you prevent crimes? Let the laws be clear and simple; let the entire force of the nation be united in their defence; let them be intended rather to favour every individual, than any particular class of man; let the laws be feared, and the laws only. The fear of the laws is salutary, but the fear of men is a fruitful and fatal source of crimes. Men enslaved, are more voluptuous, more debauched, and more cruel than those who are in a state of freedom.

Would you prevent crimes? Let liberty be attended with knowledge. As knowledge extends, the disadvantages which attend it diminish, and the advantages increase. . . . When the clouds of ignorance are dispelled by the radiance of knowledge, authority trembles, but the force of laws remains immoveable. Men of enlightened understanding must necessarily approve those useful conventions, which are the foundation of public society; they compare, with the highest satisfaction, the inconsiderable portion of liberty of which they are deprived, with the sum total sacrificed by others for their security; observing that they have only given up the pernicious liberty of injuring their fellow creatures, they bless the throne, and the laws upon which it is established.

A punishment may not be an act of violence, of one, or of many against a private member of society, it should be public, immediate and necessary; the least possible in the case given; proportional to the crimes and determined by the laws.

From Cesare Beccaria: *An Essay on Crimes and Punishments*, the fifth edition, corrected and revised, London 1801.

document 3

A PRACTICAL EDUCATION

The rejection of Original Sin and the belief that an individual's nature is formed by his environment acting through his sensations made many Enlightenment thinkers confident that mankind could be improved, if not perfected. Consequently great interest was taken in education. The reformers were united in their opposition to the traditional preoccupation with scholastic philosophy, scholastic theology and the classics but their positive proposals varied considerably. Particularly in central Europe there was great emphasis on the need for citizens useful to the state.

One must strive in the schools to educate young people in such a way that with time they become:
a. Honest Christians
b. good citizens, that is faithful and obedient subjects of the authorities; and
c. useful people for the community.

Firstly we wish to show what is meant by these terms:

Only they deserve to be called honest Christians who not only know, clearly and thoroughly, what a Christian should believe, do and not do, but who also faithfully put all this into practice and who in every situation think and act from religious motives and in accordance with religious teaching.

Good citizens (especially of a monarchical state) are all honest subjects of the sovereign; willingly and gladly a good citizen must do everything conducive to the honour and best interests of his sovereign; obey the authorities and officials placed over him by the latter, submit to their laws, orders and decisions and carry them out to the best of his ability, even if he cannot appreciate how such orders might benefit him and his fellow-citizens.

Useful people are those only who have learnt something useful and who make use of it to the benefit of themselves and other people. The teacher who is obliged to produce useful people by his instruction must teach only useful subjects and in such a way that they really can be used. Everything which cannot be applied to human existence or which at least does not help the learning of other things, is taught and learnt in vain; it is a waste of precious time. Every teacher, therefore, should examine everything he teaches and consider whether he is teaching useful subjects in such a way that they really can be used.

From Johann Ignaz Felbiger: *Eigenschaften, Wissenschaften und Bezeigen rechtschaffener Schulleute*, Bamberg und Würzburg, 1772, pp. 21–3.

THE NECESSITY OF REFORM

The humiliating defeats suffered in the War of Austrian Succession and the loss of Silesia revealed the internal decay of the Habsburg Monarchy. Its vast potential could never be realised unless what was a collection of individual provinces was turned into an unitary state. Maria Theresa's espousal of reform was dictated not by any influence of the Enlightenment but by the exigencies of the situation.

When I saw that the Peace of Dresden would have to be accepted, my way of thinking suddenly changed and turned exclusively to the internal condition of my territories, to the problem of devising means to protect the German Hereditary Lands against such powerful enemies as Prussia and Turkey, when fortresses and ready money were lacking and our armies were weak.

The role of the House of Habsburg changed completely; it could no longer think of holding the balance against France but only of its internal preservation: consequently the Netherlands and Italy were no longer reasons for prolonging the war, one had to escape from it as best one could, whatever the cost.

This was the reason for such a swift conclusion of the Peace of Aix-la-Chapelle. And after the Peace of Dresden it was my sole endeavour to learn about the condition and strength of my territories, and then to conduct a thorough examination and appraisal of the abuses which had crept into them and their organs of government, for it appeared that everything was in a state of the utmost mismanagement, confusion and chaos. Those who should have informed me about this either could not or would not.

From my own experience it was not difficult for me to appreciate that, given the situation as it had existed hitherto, the Monarchy could not have survived so long without an apparent miracle and that far less would it be able to do so in future, with such a considerable province [Silesia] lost to such a dangerous neighbour [Frederick of Prussia], who lacks neither the power nor the ambition to embark on further expansion: who because of his position is exposed to far fewer risks than I am in the event of war, because he is surrounded by far fewer neighbours: who is always prepared and who above all else rules a state which is so organised that everything he commands is not only carried out but is carried out as quickly as possible. In my territories, on the other hand, the form of government which had existed up till then was responsible for very long delays before orders were implemented. I also saw that this fundamental defect could not be rectified until the conduct of affairs was more concentrated and went through fewer hands and departments of state.

In this over-elaborate organisation of business I saw a second and far more serious defect, namely that all the official bodies saw themselves as separate entities, more concerned with the extension of their own power and prestige than with serving me, that they criticised other departments while pursuing their own interests and those of their subordinates, to the neglect of official business, that they wasted far too much time in unnecessary bickering and red tape and that they obstructed rather than assisted the implementation of my orders.

Yet the greatest defect of all was that in Bohemia and Austria the chancellors had acquired so much power that they were feared and respected almost more than the sovereign, because there was an ancient tradition of administering the two provinces by separate chancelleries, because the Bohemian chancellor was always a Bohemian and the Austrian chancellor always an Austrian and because all official ordinances were channelled through them. Consequently everything depended mainly on them. Partly to increase their prestige and their following and partly because they owned property there and sat in the estates, the chancellors gave undue support to provincial privileges, to the detriment of the sovereign's interests, and behaved as if they represented the provinces rather than the sovereign.

It followed naturally from this primary source of confusion that there was very little unity of purpose in the various departments of state, for the Austrian chancellor concentrated on the welfare and relief of Austria and the Bohemian chancellor did

125

the same for his province, without either of them considering the interests of the whole Monarchy.

It was inevitable that disunity between the chancelleries would lead to disunity between the provinces, for each chancellery sought to reduce the burden of taxation falling on their province by pushing more on to the other.

The most serious effects of this state of affairs were firstly that the chancellors concealed from the court the true internal condition of their provinces, partly to make themselves all the more indispensable to the court and partly to improve their standing with the estates, secondly that the estates were given far too much freedom in the conduct of internal affairs and in the levy of taxation, particularly in Austria, and thirdly that by paying out large sums of money to noble landowners, to themselves and for sundry other purposes, the estates heaped debt upon debt, without the central authorities exercising any kind of control over their finances. This abuse had been pushed to an almost incredible extent, so that when the new system was introduced Carinthia and Carniola alone were more than seven million gulden in debt. I was obliged to recognise the inescapable necessity of searching for a remedy, if the total decay of the Monarchy was to be arrested in time.

After careful consideration I decided that the decayed old order would have to be changed completely, at the centre and in the provinces, and that its replacement would be based firmly on the principles of systematic order.

To this end, all public, financial and military affairs were transferred from the old authorities to the newly established Directorio [in publicis et cameralibus]. The two chancelleries were abolished entirely, while the treasury retained control only of Hungary and the royal domains; it too was to perish when its president died. A Supreme Court was set up to deal with justice in all the Bohemian and Austrian Hereditary Lands.

It was easy to predict that a project of this scale, which aimed at the modification of the old constitution and the abolition of the abuses and the disorder which had existed for time out of mind, would provoke only discontent and opposition among the people, who were prejudiced against it in advance. In the event everyone did howl against it, particularly the army, the estates, the nobility and the imperial officials. But the loudest cries of protest came from the court, either from those who depended on my favour for their livelihood or from those who owed their present wealth and status to the kindness and generosity of my predecessors. For that very reason they suffered more than other groups from the abolition of intolerable abuses and the introduction of equality and order.

From Heinrich Kretschmayr: *Maria Theresa*, Gotha, 1925, pp. 232–9.

document 5
MONASTERIES ARE UNNECESSARY AND HARMFUL

Not only atheists and anticlericals but also Catholic reformers demanded restrictions on the numbers and the wealth of the monasteries. They asserted that the monks were unproductive, parasitical and superstitious. In the following extract, which contains most of the antimonastic arguments, Kaunitz comments on a report from the committee on ecclesiastical affairs.

All opinions previously expressed seem to assume that it is doubtful whether or not there are more monks than necessary. I on the other hand consider that their present number is as exaggerated as it is unnecessary and is so disadvantageous to the state and religion that failure to correct this undetected but cancerous abuse will lead inevitably to the Catholic states of Europe falling more and more into decay, and the non-Catholic states increasing more and more in power and wealth.

It seems to me that the following principles can serve as an irrefutable proof of this assertion.

As is well known, the clerical estate is dedicated to celibacy and is therefore very disadvantageous to the propagation of the human race. Those who are admitted to this estate are for the most part the pick of the citizens in physical and intellectual gifts.

They are withdrawn for all time from agriculture, from military service, from the arts and the professions, from manufacturing, and the factories, from commerce etc., in a word from almost all other useful civil occupations in society. In most

127

countries their estates and possessions are far greater than all the laity's put together and yet there is no Catholic state in which the laity, considering their numbers and the important, onerous and multifarious services they perform for society, do not bear a vastly greater fiscal burden than the clergy. Indeed in many countries the clerical estate is freed entirely from the obligation to contribute to this burden, although it enjoys all the advantages of the state's constitution. The load is borne solely by the other citizens.

In addition, because the ownership never changes, the possessions of the clergy are withdrawn from circulation, as a result of which the sovereign loses the benefits which normally accrue to him from the various transfers of property. This is not to mention the enormous part of their fortune which derives from the payments of the brotherhoods, societies and sodalities for the reading of masses, from secret donations and from other sources. Because this income cannot be checked reliably, it cannot be taxed.

It is clear therefore that the clerical estate in general and the monastic orders in particular, because their members are of both sexes, are exceedingly harmful to both the state and civil society, that they can be justified only on the grounds of necessity and that consequently *salus populi suprema legum* makes it absolutely essential that this class of citizens be reduced as much as possible.

Therefore the only question seems to be whether the present number of regular clergy of both sexes can be restricted and reduced without harming the essential interests of the Catholic religion.

It is universally known that the Church existed for more than three centuries before anyone knew anything about monks. Consequently their introduction was quite arbitrary and had nothing to do with the essence of Christianity.

Just as religion and the Church managed to exist for several centuries without the monks, indeed this being the period when they attained their greatest degree of purity and perfection, so could they now dispense entirely with the regular clergy. At all events, the many thousands of monks could be replaced by a few hundred secular clergy and priests actively concerned with the cure of souls.

Consequently it is incontrovertible that there are far too many monks, for the Church can do without them altogether.

Even if they were merely unnecessary and superfluous, their numbers would have to be reduced. This reduction becomes all the more necessary when one observes that the monks are not only useless but at the same time extremely harmful to civil society in all sorts of ways. Their number can be reduced without religion suffering the slightest harm. The wellbeing of the state demands it; and in my opinion the principles of rational legislation require that when operating on the body politic one should borrow the technique of a skilful doctor, who when confronted by a critically dangerous illness seeks primarily and immediately to prevent any aggravation of the infection. I propose therefore that all superiors of the monastic orders of both sexes be sent immediately a carefully composed ordinance ordering that: In that Your Majesty has learnt that to a greater or lesser extent the personnel of the monastic orders has exceeded the numbers established when they were admitted to the state, each of them must send in to the Chancellery within the shortest possible space of time a legally attested copy of their deeds of foundation and that from now until further notice they must neither recruit nor accept new members.

At the same time all monastic houses must be ordered to reveal the exact state of their resources to a commission set up specially for the purpose. They must be completely frank, their accounts must be supported by all the documentary evidence available and by their sacerdotal oath. In the meantime they must not dare to remove from the state even the smallest part of their possessions, on pain of confiscation and the total dissolution of the offending monastery. In my opinion these measures should be introduced immediately. All other remedies could then safely be examined and considered in greater detail. It would be superfluous therefore for me to express any opinions about them at this stage.

From Ferdinand Maass: *Der Josephinismus* . . . vol. II: *Enfaltung und Krise des Josephinismus*, 1770–1790, (**7**) pp. 139–41.

document 6
THE ABOLITION OF PERSONAL SERFDOM

Joseph opposed serfdom on the grounds of reason, humanity and economic efficiency. His abolition of personal serfdom in 1781 made the peasants free agents in a legal sense but did not affect the dues they owed their lords by virtue of the land they held. He attempted to destroy this economic subjection by the tax decree of 1789.

Henceforth serfdom in Bohemia[1] is abolished in its entirety. In its place a moderate form of subjection is introduced and the following arrangement has the force of law:

1. Every subject is entitled to marry if he announces his intention beforehand and if he fills in an official form, for which there is no charge.

2. If he observes the commercial regulations prevailing in his district, every subject is free to leave his lord's estate and to seek employment or to settle elsewhere in the province. But those subjects who leave their lords to settle on an estate elsewhere must obtain a free release certificate, to prove to their new lord that their old lord has released them from all obligations.

3. The subjects can learn the trades and professions of their choice and can pursue their livelihood where they find it without needing special papers, which moreover are abolished altogether.

4. In future no subject will be obliged to perform domestic services for his lord; except that

5. orphans are obliged to serve lords who have acted as guardians without remuneration, but the period of service must not exceed three years and can only be enforced where this arrangement is traditional.

Finally 6. all other dues incumbent on the subject, whether

[1] Similar ordinances were published for the other provinces of the Monarchy.

in the form of services, money or in kind, which derive from his tenure of the lord's land and which remain binding even after the abolition of serfdom, are fixed by the urbarial patents. Apart from these, nothing more can be demanded of the subject. However after the abolition of serfdom the subjects still owe their lords obedience, in accordance with the laws which remain in force.

From Otto Frass: *Quellenbuch zur österreichischen Geschichte*, vol. II (4), Document 4.

document 7
THE SHORTCOMINGS OF THE OFFICIALS

The success of Joseph's programme depended largely on the loyalty and efficiency of his officials. To his intense chagrin, he discovered that in their scale of priorities personal, provincial and class interests took precedence over his own. The following admonition, dated 1783, was one of many.

Three years have now passed since I took over the administration of the state. During this period, with considerable effort, care and patience, I have made my principles, opinions and intentions adequately known to all departments of state. I have not confined myself to simply issuing orders; I have expounded and explained them. With enlightenment I have sought to weaken and with arguments I have sought to overcome the abuses which had arisen out of prejudice and deeply rooted customs. I have sought to imbue every official of the state with the love I myself feel for the wellbeing of the whole and with enthusiasm for its service. It follows naturally from this that, taking oneself as a starting-point, all one's actions must be motivated by concern for the advantage and the best interests of the greatest number. I have given the heads of departments my confidence and have granted them powers not only to be effective in a purely administrative sense but also to influence the opinions of their subordinates. They have been given exclusive control of the selection of personnel. I welcomed from them, as I did from everyone, complaints supported by argument and factual reports, which are always valuable.

My doors were open to them every hour of every day, to hear their grievances and to resolve their doubts. I now consider that my duty and the loyalty to the state which I have sworn to observe in all my actions for as long as I live demand that I insist most forcibly that the principles and orders which I issue are followed and carried out without exception. I have observed with regret that up till now they have been so neglected that although a great deal has been commanded and even published very little has been done in the way of observation and execution. As a result repeated orders have to be issued, and even then one has no confidence that they will be carried out. Indeed the way in which most of the officials go about their business shows that they are not trying to promote the general good and to instruct the people about it but are doing the absolute minimum required to avoid becoming involved in an official inquiry and risking dismissal. It is impossible to conduct public business properly in this mechanical and menial fashion.

The good of the state can be understood only in general terms, only in terms of the greatest number. Similarly, all the provinces of the Monarchy constitute one whole and therefore can have only one aim. It is necessary therefore that there should be an end to all the prejudices and all the jealousies between provinces, races and even departments, which have caused so much fruitless bickering. The lesson must be well and truly learnt that the body politic is similar to the human body, in that when one part is sick the whole body suffers and all parts must contribute to the healing process, however trifling the disease. Race or religion must not make any difference in all this and all must strive to be useful to one another, as brothers in one Monarchy.

From *Vollständige Sammlung aller seit dem glorreichsten Regierungsantritt Josephs des Zweyten ... Verordnungen und Gesetze* (**14**), vol. III, Vienna, 1789, pp. 251–63.

NOBLE BRUTALITY AND MAGYAR PARTICULARISM IN HUNGARY

The most formidable opponents of Joseph's unitary state were the Magyar gentry of Hungary. Entrenched in their counties (the comitati) *they resisted stoutly attempts to abolish their rights of self-administration and their control of the peasants. The unsuccessful war against the Turks and the threat of an armed insurrection forced Joseph to revoke his administrative reforms in 1790. The imperial administration had proved to be inadequate and unreliable and not even Joseph was prepared to appeal over the heads of the nobles to the peasants.*

4th September 1784. Joseph to Leopold

You appear to be curious about the difficulties I have encountered in Hungary. It is general conscription which has been misrepresented and which the nobility have viewed with distrust. It has prompted actions and protests from the *comitati* assemblies which have exceeded all bounds of moderation and propriety. I have dismissed the Count of Forgas, who was Obergespan at Neutra and the most insolent of them all. I have sent in a commissar and a battalion of infantry, with orders to carry out the conscription and there can be no doubt that it will be carried out in its entirety. It was essential that I should stand firm on this occasion, when there was no question of wronging anyone and when there was no law in existence which opposed the introduction of conscription. On the other hand, it was an act of royal authority, to cover all cases, and they were shown that they had to yield.

As regards affairs in Transylvania, to which I have referred only briefly in my letters, I enclose the two principal reports of the commanding general, which will give you a rough picture of what is going on there. The excesses of every kind committed by the landowners for a number of years have given rise to general complaints from the entire nation, and particularly from the Wallachians. Never had it been possible to remedy this situation, not even by an urbarial law. Her late Majesty had done what one might expect. Finally I succeeded in making the government and the chancellery broach the topic but nothing was actually drawn up. The officials of the domain land of Zalathma, which are under the direction of the Department of Mines, distinguished themselves particularly by all sorts of extortions. Despite repeated complaints and despite the commissions sent there, no one succeeded in putting an end to them. At last, when I found myself in the area last year, I arranged for a new commission to be set up, which was to report directly to Vienna. A report was received in March but the Department of Mines allowed it to lie about until November. Moreover the subjects had also sent to Vienna some deputies, who had a written assurance from the Hungarian Chancellery that all they had to do was to return to their homes and wait quietly for a decision, without having anything to fear. Scarcely had they returned home than they were arrested and maltreated yet again. Then one of them, called Hora, escaped, assembled the peasants and stirred them up against the landowners and their officials, saying that what had been done to them was contrary to the orders of the Emperor; finally they claimed that their areas were incorporated in the military districts. Instead of playing down the affair and making them see reason, the commanding general ordered a commissar to round them up; the commissar even made each of them pay him a small present of money and told the priests to collect it. Then the government informed the insurgents, who refused to work for their lords because they claimed to be soldiers, that the conscription was not valid. But they rejected this, saying that it was easy to see that the Hungarian seigneurs only wanted to oppress them, against my orders. At this point they progressed to the plan of burning the castles of the landowners and chasing them out of the country, while at the same time taking care to protect the villages and anything else which belonged directly to the sovereign. The blaze spread gradually and the Wallachians, completely disaffected, sent orders from village to village, pretending that they came from me, instructing the inhabitants to wipe out the nobility. The peasants responded accordingly.

When the disorders began the provincial government and the commanding general spent five days talking about what should be done. This delay allowed the revolt to gain a foothold and to spread, with the result that a thousand disorders ensued. Finally the army was forced to suppress them, some drunks offered resistance and large numbers of people were killed. Among other things, the provincial government hit upon the wretched idea that the nobles should get together, arm themselves and their Hungarian servants and march against their Wallachian subjects. I leave you to judge what excesses they committed. Among others, they arrested thirty-seven peasants and executed them on the same day, without any kind of trial.

I have recalled the commanding general and have sent in his place General Fabris. Two commissars, one military and one civil, are to investigate the causes of the affair and are to introduce effective remedies for the peasants' grievances. The Urbarium will be published and in the meantime a general pardon should persuade the insurgents to return to their homes.

My Hungarian business is making progress, but slowly. I have assembled here five of the most distinguished legal experts to work on the establishment of a new judicial system. I shall have to make sure that they perform their task in accordance with the principles I have laid down. In the meantime a sordid investigation is being conducted into the activities of the officials of the Hungarian Chancellery here. The most deplorable things have been going on: papers have been stolen, fiscal rights have been misappropriated and the registrar has been arrested. Several witnesses are giving evidence and the Chancellor's private secretary, who knew everything, tried to cut his throat with a knife in the middle of the Chancellery. He was in no way insane. As he did so, he said: 'Learn from me how to keep secrets.' Fortunately he did not die and I have placed him under observation.

3 February 1785. Joseph to Leopold

I enclose an account of the events of the last week. They were of no great importance, except for a resolution which I sent to the Hungarian Chancellery and which refuted some of the principles on which they had based their arguments. Likewise I have appointed a number of commissars in place of the Obergespane; instead of 54 individuals who did nothing, I have appointed eight who will supervise the execution of my orders.

14 January 1786. Joseph to Leopold

You will note my resolution for Hungary,[1] which will cause something of a stir; nevertheless it is essential that it be introduced and that once and for all the Monarchy should become nothing more than a single province, with uniform organisation and an equal burden of taxation.

2 March 1786. Joseph to Leopold

I enclose a copy of the edict sent to Hungary relating to the survey and assessment of estates. This will provoke weeping and wailing but nevertheless I believe that it can be put through without any real difficulty.

21 November 1786. Joseph to Leopold

Hungarian affairs take up a great deal of my time: you know yourself what my instruments are like; I have to batter away six times at the same place to rouse these sluggards and overcome their ill-will.

16 February 1790. Leopold to Joseph

I take the liberty of sending back to you the enclosed documents. I believe that your decision on Hungary[2] is glorious and excellent; this policy alone can restore vitally needed stability to this beautiful province, especially in the present circumstances. May it please God that this will put an end to the disturbances and also that peace may be made with the Turks, so that war with the King of Prussia may be averted.

From Alfred Ritter von Arneth: *Joseph II und Leopold von Toscana. Ihr Briefwechsel von* 1781 *bis* 1790, vol. I: *1781–1785*; vol. II, *1786–1790*, Vienna, 1872.

[1] Joseph refers to a communication of 5 January 1786, which he sent t the senior Hungarian Vice-Chancellor Count Karl Palffy announcing th. introduction of the new tax system to Hungary.

[2] Leopold refers to Joseph's instruction of 28 January 1790, that the administrative system as it existed before his reforms be restored. Joseph died on 19 February.

SUPERVISION OF OFFICIALS

Joseph made every attempt to ensure that his administration was worthy of the encyclopaedic responsibilities he had entrusted to it. It is doubtful however whether his constant harrying of his ill-paid and overworked officials did anything to improve their performance. Senior officials were ordered to despatch to Vienna at regular intervals detailed information about their subordinates in the following form.

1. Office or title.
2. Christian names and surname.
3. Age.
4. Length of service.
5. Previous position.
6. Whether he is married, with or without children.
7. Whether he has private means.
8. Whether he displays in the execution of his duties exceptional, average or poor industry.
9. Whether he has any academic qualifications and what languages he speaks.
10. Whether he has knowledge of foreign countries, and if so which.
11. What he is best at.
12. Whether he leads a pious and Christian way of life.
13. Whether he shows respect and obedience to his superiors.
14. Whether he is good-natured or difficult in his dealings with other people, and whether he is bad-tempered at work.
15. Whether he is addicted to gambling, drinking, indebtedness or any other kind of vice.

From *Vollständige Sammlung aller seit dem glorreichsten Regierungsantritt Josephs des Zweyten für die k.k. Erbländer ergangenen höchsten Verordnungen und Gesetze*, vol. V, p. 191.

THE JOSEPHIST STATE-CHURCH

On 19 December 1781, Court- and State-Chancellor Kaunitz replied on behalf of Joseph II to a communication he had received from the papal nuncio, Giuseppe Garampi, on 12 December. This reply was the classic definition and justification of the Josephist Church. Kaunitz alleged that Garampi had made five objectionable statements: 1. he had asserted that certain of Joseph's ecclesiastical reforms and in particular those relating to the monasteries were to the detriment of the Catholic Church; 2. he had claimed that Joseph had abolished regular institutions of monastic houses, despite their solemn approval by the Church; 3. he had insinuated that Joseph had not behaved in a manner befitting a Catholic ruler; 4. he had envisaged the possibility of subjects withdrawing their allegiance and 5. he had claimed that Joseph had appropriated for his bishops rights which were the exclusive property of the Pope.

As regards 1: The abolition of abuses which gradually have crept into the branches of church discipline is not only not detrimental to religion but rather can lead to its advantage and consolidation.

Not a single one of the abuses can be found in the essence of the Christian religion propagated by the Apostles; they and their religion were admitted and accepted by the rulers of most civilised countries because of the moderation of their principles and the excellence of their moral teaching. One may presume that they never would have been admitted, to the eternal misfortune of mankind, if any part of their religion had encroached on the power of the ruler or had not been in the interests of good government.

The abolition of abuses which affect neither the principles of the faith nor the spirit and the soul alone can never belong to the See of Rome because, except in the two instances mentioned, it cannot exercise the slightest power within the state.

This power belongs solely and exclusively to the sovereign ruler, who enjoys the right of command in the state.

Without exception, this holds good for everything which concerns the external discipline of the clergy and particularly of the monastic orders. As is well known, the Christian Church knew nothing of the latter for several centuries and would still know nothing, had not Catholic princes seen fit to admit them, gradually and in greater or lesser numbers, into their states.

In no way do they have anything to do with faith and religion.

As is also well known, they owe their presence in states where they now exist to their voluntary and arbitrary acceptance by the princes.

It follows from these irrefutable truths that His Imperial Majesty was not only fully entitled to act as he has done in this matter but even that, in accordance with his duties as the sovereign power, he is obliged to act in future in the same manner, except in matters affecting dogma and the soul alone. And finally,

There is no need to remedy wrongs done to religion or the Church when the wrongs exist only in the imagination and anyway are completely inadmissible, as they are in the present case.

As regards 2: Encroachment on the legitimate prerogatives of another is so far removed from His Imperial Majesty's celebrated love of justice that His Majesty had not even thought of abolishing the institution of a monastic order which had been approved by the Holy See. The only conclusion to be drawn from this is that it is a matter of the utmost indifference to His Majesty whether this or that spiritual institution, which His Majesty has abolished in his own territories, continues to exist in other states or not.

But just as His Majesty would never consider impeding the Holy See in the exercise of its proper and legitimate rights – those relating to dogma and matters concerning the soul alone – so he will never allow foreign interference in matters he considers to be the indisputable preserve of the secular sovereign. This includes, without exception, everything in the Church which has been invented and instituted by man rather than God and everything which owes its existence solely to acceptance and approval by the sovereign power. The latter can and must not only modify and restrict but also even abolish entirely all such voluntary and arbitrary concessions, and others of a similar nature, whenever reasons of state, abuses or changed times and circumstances demand it.

As regards 3: His Majesty flatters himself that after more

careful consideration the Nuncio will say to himself everything that needs to be said on this point. Similarly, His Majesty anticipates that the same will apply to

Point 4, but he feels obliged to add that he would never, could never find himself in the position of ordering one of his subjects to do something which was irreconcilable with the latter's conscience and that consequently His Majesty has no fear of insurrection but on the contrary knows how to ensure obedience. However, in the unlikely event of someone feeling that because of his conscience he could not obey, he would be given complete freedom to emigrate to whichever country he chose. And finally:

As regards 5: His Majesty has ordered that the Nuncio be reminded that the rights which are the exclusive property of the Pope cannot include those which are acknowledged by everyone to have been for centuries in our most sacred religion exclusive to and indivisible from the episcopacy. Consequently, when His Majesty the Emperor instructed the bishops of his Hereditary Lands to resume the exercise of their traditional and inalienable rights, all he was doing was to abolish an abuse which had invited many criticisms and had been very detrimental to his subjects' standard of living.

A proof of the personal esteem in which His Imperial Majesty holds Papal Nuncio Garampi was his prompt order to his Court- and State-Chancellor to compose a reply, which the latter has now done so that the Nuncio will be in a position to conduct his future behaviour accordingly.

Consequently all that remains for the Court- and State-Chancellor is to assure His Excellency of his devotion.

From Ferdinand Maass: *Der Josephinismus* . . . vol. II: *Entfaltung und Krise des Josephinismus* (**7**), pp. 291–4.

REORGANISATION AND RELAXATION OF CENSORSHIP

Joseph displayed an insensitivity to personal criticism rarely found in rulers or politicians. His censorship ordinance of 1781 continued the process of relaxation begun in the previous reign. Despite the restrictions which remained, Vienna was flooded with anticlerical and pornographic works. Towards the end of the reign, as fears of revolution mounted, restrictions were reimposed.

His Majesty has found that his sovereign duty requires that an alteration be made in the existing organisation of book censorship, to make it in future easier and simpler. With this aim in view he has decreed that henceforth there shall be only one main commission for the censorship of books, which will serve all the Hereditary Lands and will be located in Vienna. It will collate decisions taken on censorship both at Vienna and in the provinces and will establish a uniform guide as to which books are allowed and which books are banned. The previous censorship commissions in the provinces will be abolished, only a department for the supervision of books will be retained and in future the administration of the regulations relating to the censorship of books in the provinces will be transferred and entrusted to the care of the individual provincial authorities. At the same time His Majesty is of the opinion that:

1. All works which contain improper scenes and absurd obscenities and which could never be conducive to learning or enlightenment are to be proceeded against with all severity, but those which do evince learning, knowledge and decent principles can be dealt with all the more leniently in that whereas the former kind are read only by the great multitude and cretins, the latter fall into the hands only of those who possess already mature intellects and steadfast principles.

2. Works which make systematic attacks on the Catholic religion and repeatedly on the Christian religion cannot be

141

tolerated. Nor can those which make the sacred religion ridiculous, thus allowing the inception and spread of atheism, or those which make it contemptible by the distortion of the powers of the Almighty and by spurious and fanatical devotional excesses.

3. Because the lover of truth must rejoice when he finds it, however it was attained, there will be no ban on works containing criticisms of personalities, whether they are directed at the sovereign or at the humblest subject, unless the attacks are libellous. This will be especially the case if the author appends his name to the piece, as a guarantee of the accuracy of the contents.

4. Series of books or periodicals are not to be prohibited because individual volumes contain objectionable passages, provided that the work as a whole is useful. In any case, it is not likely that such extensive works would fall into the hands of those on whom such passages would have a detrimental effect.

From Otto Frass: *Quellenbuch zur österreichischen Geschichte* (4), vol. III, Document 1.

document 12

THE EMANCIPATION OF THE JEWS

Like their co-religionists in most other European countries, the Jews in the Habsburg Monarchy were subjected to every kind of discrimination. By a series of ordinances promulgated in 1781 and 1782, from which the following extracts are taken, Joseph removed the worst of their disabilities. Partly he was concerned to make them more useful for the state but it is undeniable that he was also influenced by the humanitarian teaching of the Enlightenment. The rabid anti-semitism of the majority of his subjects prevented him from establishing complete parity between Jews and Christians.

In order to make the Jews more useful, the discrimination hitherto observed in relation to their clothing is abolished in its entirety. Consequently the obligation for the men to wear yellow armbands and the women to wear yellow ribbons is abolished. If they behave quietly and decently, then no one has the right to dictate to them on matters of dress.

Within two years the Jews must abandon their own language: from now on all their contracts, bonds, wills, accounts, ledgers, certificates, and everything which is binding, whether of a legal nature or not, must be drawn up in German, on pain of being declared null and void and being refused official support. Consequently the Jews may use their own language only during religious services.

The best way of ensuring the success of this could be the reform of the Jewish intermediate schools in accordance with the official educational plan, albeit under the direction of the existing school managements. However there would be not the slightest interference with the Jews' religious services or faith.

Those Jews who do not have the opportunity to send their children to Jewish schools are to be compelled to send them to Christian schools, to learn reading, writing, arithmetic and other subjects.

Jewish youths will also be allowed to attend the imperial universities.

In consideration of the decision to open to the Jews means of employment hitherto closed to them, it is granted further that:

a. The Jews may engage in agriculture, especially in the uncultivated regions, but on the following conditions: only in areas where they are settled already and not anywhere they like and the land may only be leased, must be leased for a minimum period of twenty years, so that all the work is done by the Jews, and may not be leased from subjects who pay state taxes. If they become Christians however they may also lease the property of this group. As the Jews have no experience of agriculture as yet, they may employ Christian labourers for the first few years, but must allow them to sleep in Christian homes. In pursuit of their livelihood they may acquire draught animals, and share in the common grazing rights. This last concession is conditional on the number of Jews in any community not exceeding the present figure. They will also be permitted:
b. to engage in the haulage trade, and
c. to learn all skills from Christian masters, but to practise them only in accordance with civic conventions and official ordinances. The same condition applies to:
d. the practice of painting, sculpture and the other liberal arts.

They will also be permitted:

e. to engage in manufacturing where specialised and expensive machinery is required and to engage in wholesale and overseas trade. Finally:
f. This also includes those manufactures which have been declared free,[1] that is weaving, spinning, taffeta-making and so on.

To prevent the Jewish children and the Jews in general suffering as a result of the concessions granted to them, the authorities and the leaders of the local communities must instruct the subjects in a rational manner that the Jews are to be regarded like any other fellow human-beings and that there must be an end to the prejudice and contempt which some subjects, particularly the unintelligent, have shown towards the Jewish nation and which several times in the past have led to deplorable behaviour and even criminal excesses. On the other hand the Jews must be warned to behave like decent citizens and it must be emphasised in particular that they must not allow the beneficence of His Majesty to go to their heads and indulge in wanton and licentious excesses and swindling, but that by upright behaviour as citizens of the world they must show themselves worthy of His Majesty's favour.

All personal taxes, double legal fees, pass-in, pass-out and curfew dues, which previously were required from the Jews and which distinguished them from Christians, are to be abolished and in this respect the Jews are to be treated in exactly the same way as the Christian inhabitants.

From *Vollständige Sammlung aller seit dem glorreichsten Regierungsantritt Josephs des Zweyten . . . höchsten Verordnungen und Gesetze* (**14**), vol. IV, pp. 60–83.

[1] i.e. those which had been declared exempt from guild regulations.

BAROQUE PIETY IN VIENNA

Paradoxically, some of the most vociferous opposition to Joseph's reforms came from the very classes they were intended to benefit. The conservatism of the masses was most apparent in their refusal to accept religious inno-vations. Their fervent attachment to traditional forms of worship thwarted Joseph's attempts to impose a 'pure' religion but ensured their immunity to the infection of revolutionary ideas.

The great crowd of clerical gentlemen of every kind, the great crowd of monks of every shape and form, the pictures and the worship of saints, the relics, the wonder-working shrines and their alleged miracles, the masses, the transubstantiations, the blessings, the litanies, the pilgrimages, processions and funerals, the brotherhoods of so many different kinds, the prayers and devotions, part of which are directed at very strange objects, the confessions, the indulgences, the penances, the mortifica-tion, the fasting, the making of the sign of the cross, the rolling of eyes, the beating of breasts, the mechanical jabbering of prayers, the scapularies, the girdles and vestments, the illumina-tions and music, spraying with holy water, the rosaries, the greeting with: Praised be Jesus Christ, the continual ringing of bells; and who knows what else that belongs to spiritual Catholic pomp and to Catholic superstition: while I was in Vienna all these things struck one everywhere one went.

From Friedrich Nicolai: *Beschreibung einer Reise durch Deutschland und die Schweiz im Jahre 1781* . . . (**8**), vol. V, p. 18.

SUPERSTITION IN THE COUNTRYSIDE

The bigotry of the public in these parts [Tyrol, Styria and Carinthia], which is still to be found even amongst people of rank, degenerates among the common people into the grossest and most abominable buffoonery. The *Windes*, who are mixed with the Germans in these countries, distinguish themselves by a superstitious custom, that does little honour to the human understanding, and would be incredible, if we had not the most unequivocal proof of the fact before our eyes. Many years ago, they set out, in company with some Hungarian enthusiasts, to Cologne on the Rhine, which is about one hundred and twenty German miles distant, to cut off the beard of a crucifix there. Every seven years this operation is repeated, as in this space of time the beard grows again to its former length. The rich persons of the association send the poorer ones as their deputies, and the magistrates of Cologne receive them as ambassadors from a foreign prince. . . . These Windes have alone the right to shave Our Saviour, and the beard grows only for them. They firmly believe, that if they did not do this service to the crucifix, the earth would be shut to them for the next seven years, and there would be no harvests. For this reason they are obliged to carry the hair home with them, as the proof of having fulfilled their commission, the returns of which are distributed amongst the different communities, and preserved as holy reliques. . . . I could give you still more striking traits of the superstition of the inhabitants of the inner parts of Austria, but as this surpasses them all, it may serve as a sufficient measure of the human understanding in these parts.

From J. C. Riesbeck: *Travels Through Germany* . . . trans. Maty (**11**), vol. I, pp. 81–3.

document 15

COUNTER REVOLUTION IN BELGIUM

Nowhere was Joseph's attempt to impose a blueprint from above more disastrous than in Belgium. Opposition from the vested interests to attempts to destroy their privileges was joined to the clerical fervour of the intensely pious population. By the end of 1789 the Austrians had been ejected from the country. The great majority of the insurgents wished only to restore the situation as it had existed before Joseph began his reforms; it was he who was the revolutionary.

Sire, all is lost and you have brought it on yourself; the Belgians have escaped from your rule: rightly incensed by your conduct towards them, they have thrown off the yoke which a cruel and irresponsible minister[1] had imposed on them; and with the clear assistance of the Almighty only a few warriors from amongst them were needed to demolish entirely the edifice of despotism. Indeed, at Turnhout, a very small number was seen to repulse the frenzied attacks of Schroeder, although he had three times as many troops; so that your general, who had believed that victory was absolutely certain, was forced to flee hell for leather from the battlefield to escape death.

It was much worse at Ghent, where eight hundred fought for three days against two generals at the head of five battalions; but all this even was only a prelude to the Brussels affair; Brussels! missing the flower of its youth, who had gone to rejoin the army of the courageous Citizen de Menin; Brussels, I say, made do with three hundred badly armed heroes to attack and scatter your Richard the Lion-Heart[2] or rather the Hare-Heart, who quaked with fear although he commanded five thousand men and more than thirty pieces of cannon and who believed himself to be safe only when he was sitting in his carriage surrounded by his wine cellar, packed into crates, as, Sire, he abandoned your treasury and war chest . . .. Yes, Sire, it is to him, it is to d'Alton that you ought to attribute the loss of your Belgian provinces; it is to this savage and ignorant man, it is to his false blustering that you owe the hatred which the word 'German' inspires in the Belgians; similarly it is to the false policies of your minister, to the impetuosity of his despatches, to the intrigues which he has used to expose everything that you should ascribe the general discontent and the suspicious reaction to all his later promises. I know, Sire, that the foreigners were not the only culpable ones; I know that it is possible that initially it was a Le Clercq, a Reus and a Le Plat who drew up the reforms detested by all the estates but I believe that it was up to you to accept them or not. You could have judged the tree by observing its bark. . . . And finally, Sire, why listen to the enemies of your Belgian Church? She who has always

---

[1] Ferdinand Count von Trauttmansdorff.
[2] Richard d'Alton.

attracted the respect and admiration of all Europe; why, I say, allow the persecution of priests who are so virtuous? Why insist on the project of packing in the theologians at Louvain, like sardines? Was it worthy of an Emperor and King to interfere with the processions, with the brotherhoods? Was it worthy of an Apostolic Majesty to dissolve convents, overturn altars, ruin monasteries and have the Lord's Anointed arrested? No, Sire, no, posterity will never believe that a king who flaunted his philosophism violated twice his oath before the entire world; that in 1788 an alleged friend of humanity allowed his troops to fire indiscriminately at his innocent, peaceful and unarmed subjects; and that he who proclaimed feelings of paternal benevolence for these same subjects rewarded the perpetrators of these cold-blooded murders. Ah! Sire, you have lost the Netherlands, but the fault is yours alone.

From the *Depêche officielle de la Vérité à Joseph II, en lui annonçant la Révolution des Pays Bas*. Signed La Vèirté and dated 12 December 1789.

document 16

VIENNA THE RESIDENTIAL CITY

Unlike Paris, Vienna owed its prosperity primarily to the presence of the establishments of the nobility. The enormous sums of money they collected from their estates in the provinces and spent in the capital created a strong demand for luxury goods, service industries and domestic servants. In terms of national prosperity, this capital would have been better employed in agriculture, commerce or manufacturing goods for export rather than internal consumption but it did ensure that a revolutionary situation of the French variety did not develop.

As you know, there are twelve princely establishments in Vienna, each of which has an average annual expenditure of probably 200,000 imperial gulden; some of them, such as the Liechtensteins, Esterhazys, Schwarzenbergs, Dietrichsteins, Lobkowitzs and Grassalkowiczs put from 300,000 to 700,000 gulden into circulation. The other less wealthy establishments consume between 80,000 and 150,000.

After the princes comes a far greater number of counts'

establishments, which account for between 50,000 and 80,000 gulden per annum, and then a larger number again, which account for between 20,000 and 50,000. Other families which were elevated to baronal status under Maria Theresa used the long wars of her reign to amass large fortunes through commerce, supply contracts and divers other undertakings and now enjoy them in peace and comfort. Finally there are the establishments of the agents, financiers and merchants, whose annual expenditure runs to 10,000 and 12,000 gulden.

I have taken as an example not one of the grandest but one of the middling establishments, comparable in scale to that of one of the wealthiest counts.

If this family did not have its own establishment in the city, it could not rent one for less than 5,000 gulden.

The lady of the house needs for her service one or two chambermaids, a man servant, a washerwoman, two parlourmaids, an extra girl, a porter, a messenger and two general servants.

The man of the house has a secretary, two valets de chambre, a lackey, huntsmen, messengers, footmen, two general servants.

For the general service of the house there are a major domo, a waiter, two charwomen, two house-boys and a porter or gate-keeper.

In the kitchen there are a chef, a confectioner, a pastry-cook, a roasts-cook, plus the usual crowd of kitchen-boys, kitchen-porters, washers-up, scullery-maids etc.

The stables are looked after by a master of the horses, a riding-master, two coach-men, two postillions, two outriders, two grooms, four stable lads etc. There are also a state carriage, two travelling carriages, several horses for the travelling carriages and the barouches, 5–6 riding horses, 3–4 hacks, some draught-horses etc.

Three tables are laid every day: the master's table, the officers' table and the servants' table.

The most remunerative posts are those of the major domo and the chef, who usually is also called the *contrôleur*. They buy the requirements of the household and run the accounts; the great lords of Vienna are generous and the examination of the accounts is neither frequent nor strict.

The total number of male and female domestic servants in Vienna is estimated to be 20,000 and this estimate is certainly not exaggerated.

If the great establishments reduce their expenditure and their retinue then they also reduce the turn-over of natural and manufactured products, which in turn reduce the number and employment of the producers, and so on.

I am firmly convinced that the court and the general public should be grateful for the fact that their existence continues to be based on the great establishments.

From Joseph Pezzl: *Skizze von Wien* (9), vol. I, chapter 38.

KAUNITZ'S ADVICE TO LEOPOLD II

Joseph was so impatient and uncompromising that he alienated every section of society that might have been able to give him effective support. The following analysis by Kaunitz of his personality and methods is merciless but fair. Kaunitz agreed with most of Joseph's domestic policies but appreciated that the opposition, however selfish its interests, could not be simply ignored.

Your subjects will feel entitled to judge your personal character and your moral principles from your first actions in the first moments of your reign; and it is of the utmost importance that this impression should be favourable, because it can and will have considerable influence on the subsequent fate of your reign.

This lesson was taught by the unfortunate example of the reign of the late Joseph II. Despite all his great qualities, he had the misfortune to attract the hatred and distrust not only of his subjects but of almost every European power, because his first actions and those which followed them prompted an adverse judgment of his personal character and moral principles.

Harshness, exaggerated severity, over-hasty decisions, despotic behaviour, obsession with innovations, contempt for—even abuse of—other courts, behaviour which was not always in accordance with the demands of justice, ambitious projects which advertised hazardous aims or which gave cause for alarm aroused everywhere antipathy and distrust. His lack of resolution when he encountered real opposition aroused scorn and contempt; on the other hand, when the opposition was not really formidable, no counter-proposals could alter His Majesty's decisions, decisions which he had arrived at without first consulting anyone, indeed without himself giving them careful and dispassionate consideration.

Hinc Lacrimae. This kind of behaviour was responsible for everything that happened during the reign of a man who in

151

other respects was so great and will be responsible for what one fears will happen if immediate action is not taken to check present disorders and prevent them in future. The candid description which I have just given makes this absolutely clear and also demonstrates the necessity of applying the appropriate remedies forthwith. The latter can be nothing less than the opposite of what happened or failed to happen under the previous regime.

Without delay Your Majesty must convince all the other European states and sovereigns that you are a just, fair, moderate, warmhearted and friendly monarch, whose objectives are in no way dangerous, you must try to earn their friendship and trust in every way possible and you must try to reclaim the friendship, trust and love of your subjects, whatever their nationality, if you wish to have the pleasure of seeing internal stability secured and the desired prestige of the Austrian Monarchy restored. To this end it is essential that whatever can be done now must not be delayed and whatever cannot be done straightaway must be prepared.

The ensurance of internal stability must surely fall into this first category, as must the retention of the House of Austria's current system of alliances, until time and circumstances shall make some sort of modification necessary. As regards the first of these two important matters it is my opinion that nothing would be more appropriate than to adopt in each and every part of the Monarchy the same measures which the late emperor so admirably introduced in the Kingdom of Hungary,[1] in so far as it is possible, according to circumstances and on your own initiative, without waiting for complaints and representations. This could be done by a directive, composed according to circumstance, to each province of the Austrian Monarchy on the lines of the draft enclosed as appendix A.[2] However, to avoid the dangers which arise out of a general National Assembly, the best plan would be to summon the provincial deputations to Vienna one at a time, to listen to them and then they could be sent home

[1] This refers to Joseph II's revocation of his administrative reforms in Hungary on 28 January 1790.

[2] This appendix has not survived. Kaunitz refers to the deputations which were to be sent to Vienna by the various provincial estates to present remonstrances.

one at a time, quiet and satisfied according to the nature of their representations.

From Karl Otmar Freiherr von Aretin: *Heiliges Römisches Reich, 1776–1806 Reichsverfassung und Staatssouveränität*, Teil II: *Ausgewählte Aktenstücke, Bibliographie, Register*, Wiesbaden 1967, p. 204.

document 18

LEOPOLD AND THE CONSTITUTION

Leopold's approach to politics was diametrically opposed to that of his brother. He rejected personal absolutism, however enlightened, and insisted on the need for representative assemblies. Consequently, his abandonment of Joseph's unitary state should be seen not so much as a concession to the vested interests but rather as a consistent implementation of his political philosophy. He composed the following statement when the project of a constitution for the Grand Duchy of Tuscany was being discussed in 1782.

A constitution is useful and convenient for the sovereign, the departments of state and the officials because it clearly defines their powers and one knows what one must, may and may not do. It enables the sovereign to give an account of himself and his actions to the public at all times, so that they can see how he behaves and how he is accountable to the representatives of the estates; it enables him to see his actions always justified in the eyes of the entire public, so that they cannot do him an injustice; it frees him from all the hatred and discontent which the public levels at the activities of the officials, who are always being accused of despotism, partiality and self-interest, albeit often unjustly; and because his actions are now public he regains the confidence of the public, who otherwise always distrust government activity, look for ulterior motives and pass hostile judgments even on the good policies; it frees the sovereign from having to be responsible for the most important and complex affairs of state, that is those concerned with the alteration of the system and which are always the most difficult; it gives him the opportunity and the chance to keep his ministers and his officials up to their duty with all severity and because it makes all his actions clear and public it removes from him all hatred, suspicion and distrust, it removes the ability to do evil and leaves only the ability to do good, it allows him to make himself popular with the public through his proposals for their benefit and it allows him to demonstrate his good intentions and his good heart, whereas the estates must bear the blame if his proposals are not accepted or followed. It provides him with a great degree of stability, security and peace. It offers him the advantage of conferring with the representatives of the estates and of hearing their opinions on his proposals or changes and because they are among those whose interests are most affected and the most enlightened, it gives him the chance of obtaining fresh insights and of correcting his own ideas. An additional advantage is that while the public normally detest all changes and innovations those which he makes with the consent and approval of the estates will always be welcome, or at least the public will already be prepared and inclined to accept them and to cooperate. It ensures for the good prince the opportunity and the means to gain honour and to use his gifts for the benefit of the public, while it keeps a bad prince on such a tight reign that it prevents him from doing evil, by denying him both the opportunity and the power; it exposes him immediately to the public and forces him to become good or to appear good and to curb his passions and vices, or at least it stops him doing harm to society or serving the whims of himself, his ministers or his friends; it secures the property and prosperity of the entire public and finally it ensures contentment and peace for all sections of society.

From Adam Wandruszka: *Leopold II* (110), vol. I, pp. 377–8

Bibliography

This book has been based largely on works written in German. Because they are often unavailable and because a working knowledge of the language is seldom encountered amongst British students, most of them have been omitted from the bibliography.

I. DOCUMENTS AND CONTEMPORARY ACCOUNTS

1 Andrews, Stuart (ed.), *Enlightened Despotism*, Longmans 1967.

2 Arneth, Alfred von, *Joseph II und Leopold von Toscana, Ihr Briefwechsel*, Vienna 1872.

3 Arneth, Alfred von, *Maria Theresia und Joseph II, Ihre Correspondenz*, Vienna 1867.

4 Frass, Otto, *Quellenbuch zur österreichischen Geschichte*, vol. II, Vienna 1959.

5 Hermann, Benedict Franz, *Reisen durch Oesterreich, Steyermark, Kärnten, Krayn, Italien, Tyrol, Salzburg und Bayern im Jahre 1780. In Briefen*, 3 vols. Vienna 1781–3.

6 Lively, J., *The Enlightenment*, Longmans 1966.

7 Maass, Ferdinand, *Der Josephinismus. Quellen zu seiner Geschichte in Oesterreich 1760–1790 .Amtliche Dokumente aus dem Wiener Haus-, Hof- und Staatsarchiv*, vol. II: *Entfaltung und Krise des Josephinismus 1770–1790*, Vienna 1953.

8 Nicolai, C. F., *Beschreibung einer Reise durch Deutschland und die Schweiz im Jahre 1781. Nebst Bemerkungen über Gelehrsamkeit, Industrie, Religion und Sitten*, vol. V, Berlin and Stettin 1785.

9 Pezzl, J., *Skizze von Wien unter der Regierung Joseph II*, Vienna 1789.

10 Pichler, Caroline, *Denkwürdigkeiten aus meinem Leben*, 4 vols, Vienna 1884.

11 Riesbeck, J. C., *Travels through Germany in a series of letters, written in German and trans. by Rev. Mr Maty*, 3 vols, London 1787.

12 Rowen, H. H. (ed.), *From Absolutism to Revolution 1648–1848*, New York, Macmillan 1963.

155

13 Rudé, G. (ed.), *The Eighteenth Century*, New York, Free Press 1965.

14 *Vollständige Sammlung aller seit dem glorreichsten Regierungsantritt Josephs des Zweyten für die k.k. Erbländer ergangenen höchsten Verordnungen und Gesetze*, Vienna 1788–

15 Walter, F., *Maria Theresia: Briefe und Aktenstücke in Auswahl*, Darmstadt 1968.

II. THE ENLIGHTENMENT

16 Beccaria, Cesare, *An Essay on Crime and Punishment*, London 1801.

17 Becker, Carl L., *The Heavenly City of the Eighteenth-Century Philosophers*, Yale U.P., 1932.

18 Cassirer, E., *The Philosophy of the Enlightenment*, Princeton U.P. 1951.

19 Cobban, Alfred, *In Search of Humanity*, Cape 1960.

20 Diderot, Denis, *Œuvres Politiques*, Paris, Classiques Garnier 1963.

21 Emerson, R., 'Peter Gay and the Heavenly City', *Journal of the History of Ideas*, vol. XXVIII, 1967.

22 Epstein, Klaus, *The Genesis of German Conservatism*, Princeton U.P. 1966.

23 Gay, Peter, *The Enlightenment, an Interpretation*, vol. I: *The Rise of Modern Paganism*, Weidenfeld & Nicolson 1967.

24 Gay. Peter, 'The Enlightenment in the history of political theory', *Political Science Quarterly*, vol. LXIX, 1954.

25 Gay, Peter, *The Party of Humanity, Studies in the French Enlightenment*, Weidenfeld & Nicolson, 1964.

26 Gay, Peter, *Voltaire's Politics*, Vintage Books, n.d.

27 Hampson, Norman, *The Enlightenment*, Penguin Books 1968.

28 Hazard, Paul, *The European Mind* 1680–1715, Penguin Books 1964.

29 Hazard, Paul, *European Thought in the Eighteenth Century*. Penguin Books 1965.

30 Hertz, F., *The Development of the German Public Mind*, vol. II: *The Age of Enlightenment*, Allen & Unwin 1962.

31 Johnson, H. C., 'The concept of bureaucracy in cameralism', *Political Science Quarterly*, vol. LXIX, 1964.

32 Kant, I., 'What is Enlightenment?', in C. J. Friedrich, ed., *The Philosophy of Kant*, Random House, New York 1955.

156

33 Krieger, Leonhard, *The German Idea of Freedom, History of a Political Tradition*, Boston, Beacon Press 1957.

34 Lough, J., (ed.), *The Encyclopédie of Diderot and D'Alembert*, Cambridge U.P. 1954.

35 Mathiez, A. 'Les doctrines politiques des physiocrates', *Annales hist. de la révolution française*, no. 3, 1936.

36 Mathiez, A., 'Les philosophes et le pouvoir au milieu du XVIIIe siècle', *Annales hist. de la révolution française*, no. 1, 1935.

37 Mauzi, R., *L'Idée du bonheur au XVIII siècle*, Paris 1960.

38 Montesquieu, Baron de, *The Spirit of the Laws*, trans. by Thomas Nugent, New York, Hafner 1966.

39 Palmer, R. R., *Catholics and Unbelievers in Eighteenth-Century France*, Princeton U.P. 1949.

40 Price, K. B., 'Cassirer and the Enlightenment', *Journal of the History of Ideas*, vol. XVIII, 1957.

41 Rolland, R., Maurois, A., and Herriot, E., (ed.), *French Thought in the Eighteenth Century*, Cassell 1953.

42 Rothkrug, H., *The Opposition to Louis XIV, The Origins of the French Enlightenment*, Princeton U.P. 1966.

43 Rousseau, J. J., *The Social Contract*.

44 Small, A. W. *The Cameralists*, New York, B. Franklin 1962.

45 Sonnenfels, J. von, *Grundsätze der Polizey, Handlung und Finanzwissenschaft. 5te vermehrte und verbesserte Auflage*, 3 vols., Vienna 1787.

46 Voltaire, *Candide*.

47 Voltaire, *Dictionnaire Philosophique*.

48 Voltaire, *Lettres Philosophiques*.

49 Voltaire, *Traité sur la Tolérance*.

50 Weulersse, G., *Le Mouvement Physiocratique en France de 1756 à 1770*, Paris 1910.

51 Wolff, Christian, *Vernünftige Gedanken von dem gesellschaftlichen Leben der Menschen*, Halle 1753.

III. ENLIGHTENED DESPOTISM AND GENERAL HISTORIES OF THE EIGHTEENTH CENTURY

52 Anderson, M. S., *Europe in the Eighteenth Century, 1713–1783*, Longmans 1961.

53 Behrens, C. B. A., *The Ancien Regime*, Thames & Hudson 1967.

54 Cragg, G., *The Church in the Age of Reason*, Penguin Books 1960.

55 Deinhardt, W., *Der Jansenismus in deutschen Landen*, Münchener Studien zur historischen Theologie, Munich 1927.

56 Dorn, W. L., *Competition for Empire, 1740–1763*, New York, Harper, 1940.

57 Droz, J., *L'Allemagne et la Révolution Française*, Paris 1949.

58 Gagliardo, J. G., *Enlightened Despotism*, Routledge & Kegan Paul 1968.

59 Gazier, A., *Histoire Générale du Mouvement Janséniste*, Paris 1922.

60 Gershoy, L., *From Despotism to Revolution, 1763–1789*, New York, Harper 1944.

61 Gooch, G. P., *Germany and the French Revolution*, Cass 1965.

62 Goodwin, A., (ed.), *The European Nobility in the Eighteenth Century*, Black 1953.

63 Godechot, J., *La Grande Nation: L'Expansion Révolutionnaire dans le monde*, 1789–99, 2 vols., Paris 1956.

64 Godechot, J., *Les Révolutions, 1770–99*, Nouvelle Clio no. 36, Paris 1965.

65 Hales, E. E. Y., *Revolution and Papacy*, 1769–1846, Eyre & Spottiswoode 1960.

66 Hempel, E., *Baroque Art and Architecture in Central Europe*, Pelican Books 1965.

67 Lefèbvre, G., 'Le Despotisme Éclairé', in *Annales de la révolution française*, no. 114, 1949.

68 Morazé, G., 'Finance et Despotisme, essai sur les despotes éclairés', *Annales, Economies, Sociétés et Civilisations*, vol. III, 1948.

69 Mousnier, R. and F. Hartung, *Quelques problèmes concernant la monarchie absolue. Relazioni del X. Congresso Internationale di Scienze Storiche*, vol. IV, *Storia Moderna*. Biblioteca Storica Sansoni Nuova Serie, vol. XXV, Florence 1955.

70 Mousnier, R. and E. Labrousse, *Histoire Générale des Civilisations*, Paris 1955.

71 *New Cambridge Modern History*, vol. VIII, Cambridge U.P., 1965.

72 Palmer, R. R. *The Age of Democratic Revolution*, 2 vols. Princeton U.P. 1959, 1964.

73 Parry, G., 'Enlightened government and its critics in eighteenth-century Germany', *The Historical Journal*, VI, 2, 1963.

74 Preclin, E. and Jarry, E., *Les Luttes Politiques et Doctrinales au XVIIe et XVIIIe Siècles: Histoire de l'église*, ed. A. Fliche and V. Martin, vol. XIX, Paris 1955.

75 Preclin, E., 'L'influence du jansénisme français à l'etranger', *Revue Historique*, clxxxii, 1938.

76 Ramm, Agatha, *Germany 1789–1919*, Methuen 1967.

77 Rudé, George, *Revolutionary Europe*, Collins 1964.

78 Réau, L. *L'Europe française au siècle des lumières*, Paris 1951.

79 Voltelini, H. von, 'Die naturrechtlichen Lehren und die Reformen des 18. Jahrhunderts', *Historische Zeitschrift*, CV, 1910.

80 White, R. J. *Europe in the Eighteenth Century*, Macmillan 1965.

81 Zeller, G. *Histoires des relations internationales. Les temps modernes*, Pt 2: *De Louis XIV à 1789*, Paris 1953.

IV. THE HABSBURG MONARCHY

82 Arneth, Alfred von, *Geschichte Maria Theresias*, 10 vols., Vienna 1863–79.

83 Bernard, Paul, *Joseph II and Bavaria. Two attempts at German unification*, The Hague 1965.

84 Blum, Jerome, *Noble Landowners and Agriculture in Austria, 1815–1848, A study in the origins of the emancipation of 1848*. The Johns Hopkins University Studies in Historical and Political Science, series lxv, no. 2, Baltimore 1949.

85 Fejtö, F., *Un Habsbourg révolutionnaire, Joseph II*, Paris 1953.

86 Freudenberger, H., 'Industrialisation in Bohemia and Moravia in the eighteenth century', *Journal of Central European Affairs*, XIX, January 1960.

87 Freudenberger, H., 'The woollen goods industry of the Habsburg Monarchy in the Eighteenth Century', *Journal of Economic History*, XX, 1960.

88 Gooch, G. P., *Maria Theresa and Other Studies*, Longmans 1951.

89 Jaszi, O., *The Dissolution of the Habsburg Monarchy*, Chicago U.P. 1929.

90 Kann, R. A., *A Study in Austrian Intellectual History, from Late Baroque to Romanticism*, Thames & Hudson 1960.

91 Kerner, R. J., *Bohemia in the Eighteenth Century*, London, Macmillan 1932.

92 Klima, A., 'Industrial development in Bohemia, 1648–1781', *Past and Present*, XI, 1957.

93 Limoli, D. A., 'Pietro Verri. A Lombard reformer under Enlightened Absolutism and the French Revolution', *Journal of Central European Affairs*, XVIII, October 1958.

94 Macartney, C. A., *The Habsburg Empire 1790–1918*. Weidenfeld & Nicolson 1969.

95 Link, E. M., *The Emancipation of the Austrian Peasant*, 1740–1798, Columbia University Studies in History, Economics and Public Law, 544, New York 1949.

96 Lütge, F., (ed.), *Die wirtschaftliche Situation in Deutschland und Oesterreich um die Wende vom 18. zum 19. Jahrhundert*, Stuttgart 1964.

97 Marczali, H., *Hungary in the Eighteenth Century*, Cambridge U.P. 1910.

98 Mikoletzky, H. L., *Oesterreich—Das grosse Jahrhundert*, Vienna 1967.

99 Mitrofanov, P. von, *Joseph II, seine politische und kulturelle Tätigkeit*, Vienna 1910.

100 Padover, S. K., *The Revolutionary Emperor—Joseph II of Austria*, Eyre & Spottiswoode 1967.

101 Schünemann, K., 'Die Wirtschaftspolitik Josephs II in der Zeit seiner Mitregentenschaft', *Mitteilungen des oesterreichischen Instituts für Geschichtsforschung*, XLVII 1933.

102 Silagi, D., *Jakobiner in der Habsburger Monarchie*, Vienna and Munich 1962.

103 Stoye, J. W., 'Emperor Charles VI, the early years of his reign', *Trans. Royal Historical Society*, 5th ser. xii, 1962.

104 Strakosch, H., *State Absolutism and the Rule of Law*, Sydney U.P. 1967.

105 Sugar, P. F. 'The influence of the Enlightenment and the French Revolution in eighteenth-century Hungary', *Journal of Central European Affairs*, XVII.

106 Tassier, S., '*Les démocratesbelges de 1789: étude sur le Vonckisme et la révolution brabançonne*', Brussels 1930, in *Mémoires de l'Académie royale de Belgique, Classe des lettres*, 2nd ser., XXVIII.

107 Temperley, H. W. V., *Frederic the Great and Kaiser Joseph*, Cass 1968.

108 Valjavec, F., *Der Josephinismus. Zur geistigen Entwicklung Oesterreichs im achtzehnten und neunzehnten Jahrhundert*, Munich 1945.

109 Valsecchi, F., 'Joseph II und die Verwaltungsreform in der Lombardei', *Historica*, Vienna 1965.

110 Wandruszka, Adam, *Leopold II*, 2 vols, Vienna and Munich 1965.

111 Wangermann, E., *From Joseph II to the Jacobin Trials*, Oxford U.P. 1959.
112 Winter, E., *Der Josefinismus, Die Geschichte des oesterreichischen Reformkatholizismus*, 1740–1848, Berlin 1962.
113 Wright W., *Agrarian Reform in Eighteenth-Century Bohemia*, Minnesota U.P. 1966.

V. OTHER STATES

114 Blum, J., *Lord and Peasant in Russia from the Ninth to the Nineteenth Century*, Princeton U.P. 1961.
115 Brückner, A., *Katharina die Zweite*, Berlin 1883.
116 Bruford, W. H., *Germany in the Eighteenth Century*, Cambridge U.P. 1965.
117 Carsten, F. L., *The Origins of Prussia*, Oxford U.P. 1955.
118 Carsten, F. L., 'Prussian Despotism at its height', in *History*, XL, 1956.
119 Carsten, F. L., *Princes and Parliaments, From the Fifteenth to the Eighteenth Centuries*, Oxford U.P. 1959.
120 Cheke, M., *Dictator of Portugal—Life of the Marquis of Pombal*, Sidgwick & Jackson 1938.
121 Confino, M., *Domaines et Seigneurs en Russie vers la fin du XVIIIe siècle*, Paris 1963.
122 Diderot, Denis, *Mémoires pour Catherine II*, Paris, Classiques Garnier 1966.
123 Dorn, W. L., 'The Prussian Bureaucracy in the Eighteenth Century', *Political Science Quarterly*, xlvi, 1931, 403–23, and xlvii, 1932, 75–94 and 259–73.
124 Dorwart, R. A., *The Administrative Reforms of Frederick William I*, Cambridge, Mass., 1953.
125 Dukes, P., *Catherine the Great and the Russian Nobility*, Cambridge U.P. 1967.
126 Ergang, R. R., *The Potsdam Führer, Frederick William I*, New York, Columbia U.P. 1941.
127 Gooch, G. P., *Catherine the Great and Other Studies*, Longmans 1954.
128 Hauben, P. J., 'Pablo de Olavide and disunity in the Spanish Enlightenment', *The Historical Journal*, VIII, 1, 1965.
129 Henderson, W. O., *Studies in the Economic Policy of Frederick the Great*, Cass 1963.

130 Herr, R., *The Eighteenth-century Revolution in Spain*, Princeton U.P. 1958.
131 Hintze, Otto, *Die Hohenzollern und Ihr Werk*, Berlin 1916.
132 Holborn, H., *A History of Modern Germany*, vol. II: 1648–1840, Eyre & Spottiswoode 1965.
133 Horn, D. B., *Frederick the Great and the Rise of Prussia*, English Universities Press 1964.
134 Kahan, A., 'Continuity in economic activity and policy in the post-Petrine period in Russia', *Journal of Economic History*, XXV, 1965.
135 Klyuchevsky, V., *A History of Russia*, vol. V, London, Dent 1931.
136 Lang, D. M., *The First Russian Radical, Alexander Radishchev* (1749–1802), Allen & Unwin 1959.
137 Laran, M., 'Nobles et paysans en Russie, de "l'âge d'or" du servage à son abolition (1762–1861)', *Annales, Economies, Sociétés et Civilisations*, XXI, no. 1, 1966.
138 Mavor, J., *An Economic History of Russia*, London 1925.
139 Portal, R., 'Manufactures et classes sociales en Russie au XVIIIe siècle', in *Revue Historique*, CCI, 1949 and CCII, 1949.
140 Putnam, P., (ed.), *Seven Britons in Imperial Russia, 1692–1812*, Princeton U.P. 1952.
141 Radishchev, A. N., *Journey from St Petersburg to Moscow*, trans. by L. Wiener, Harvard U.P. 1958.
142 Raeff, M., *Plans for Political Reform in Imperial Russia, 1698–1812*, New Jersey, Prentice-Hall 1966.
143 Raeff, M., *Origins of Russian Intelligentsia—the Eighteenth-Century Nobility*, New York, Harcourt 1966.
144 Reddaway, W. F., (ed.), *Documents of Catherine the Great—the correspondence with Voltaire and the Instruction of* 1767, Cambridge U.P. 1931.
145 Ritter, G., *Frederick the Great, An Historical Profile*, Eyre & Spottiswoode 1968.
146 Rogger, H., *National Consciousness in Eighteenth-Century Russia*, Harvard U.P. 1960.
147 Rosenberg, H., *Bureaucracy, Aristocracy and Autocracy—The Prussian Experience, 1660–1815*, Harvard U.P. 1958.
148 Sarrailh, J., *L'Espagne éclairée de la seconde moitié du XVIIIe siècle*, Paris 1954.
149 Schmidt, S. O., 'La politique interieure du Tsarisme au milieu

du XVIIIe siècle', *Annales, Economies, Sociétés et Civilisations*, XXI, no. 1, 1966.

150 Scott Thomson, G., *Catherine the Great and the Expansion of Russia*, English Universities Press 1947.

151 Tooke, William, *View of the Russian Empire, during the reign of Catherine the Second and to the close of the eighteenth century*, London 1800.

152 Volz, G. B., *Die politischen Testamente Friedrichs des Grossen*, Berlin 1920.

153 Wagner, F., 'Friedrich Wilhelm I', *Historische Zeitschrift*, CLXXXI 1956.

Index

Index

Gianni, Francesco Maria, 112
Goethe, Johann Wolfgang von, 19, 91
Görz and Gradizka, 25, 46, 48
Grimm, Baron Friedrich Melchior von, 99, 103
Grotius, Hugo, 12
guilds, 6, 37, 38, 51, 63, 65, 81, 113

Häen, Anton de, 30
Haugwitz, Count Friedrich Wilhelm von, 24, 25, 29
Herzan, Cardinal, 33
Hildebrandt, Lukas, 22–3
Hontheim, Nikolaus von ['Febronius'], 58
Hörnigk, Philipp Wilhelm von, 21
Hume, David, 7
Hungary, 21, 22, 23, 25, 27–8, 35, 46–8, 54, 56, 57, 62, 64, 69, 73, 74–6, 79, 86, 88, 89, 90, 109, 114, 115, 126, 133–6, 152

Isabel of Parma, 43
Ivan VI, Emperor of Russia, 101

Jacobin Conspiracy, 88
Jansenism, 30, 34, 59, 61–2, 80
Jekaterinoslav, 105
Jesuits, 16, 30, 31, 67
Jews, 29, 66–7, 142–4
Josepha of Bavaria, 44
Joseph II, Holy Roman Emperor,
  and Maria Theresa, 39–40, 83
  character, 43, 73, 77, 86, 113, 116, 151–2
  political philosophy, 44–6
  and the administration, 46
  and Hungary, 47–8, 73–6
  and Belgium, 48–9, 73, 76–7, 83
  and Milan, 49–51
  and serfdom, 52–3, 109
  and the nobility, 109
  and the economy, 54–7
  and the Church, 58–63
  and religious toleration, 64–7
  and censorship, 67
  and education, 68–9
  and law reform, 69–70, 120
  and social welfare, 70–2
  and provincialism, 73–4
  and his officials, 78–80
  and popular conservatism, 80–2
  and foreign policy, 82–6, 151–3
  and opposition in the Monarchy, 86–91

and Frederick the Great, 95–8
and Catherine the Great, 103–6, 109–10
his influence on other states, 111–112
and Leopold II, 43, 151–2
Josephism, 34–5, 45, 80
Justi, Johann Heinrich Gottlob von, 15

Kant, Immanuel, 16, 17, 39
Kaunitz, Wenzel Anton Prince, 26–7, 29, 30, 33–5, 38, 39, 40, 58, 59, 83, 84, 85, 127–9, 137–40, 151–3

law reform, 37–9, 69–70, 74, 88, 96, 113, 120–2, 135
League of Princes, 84
Leibniz, Gottfried Wilhelm von, 4
Leopold II, Holy Roman Emperor, 43, 76, 85, 112–16, 151–4
Liège, 77
Loudon, Marshal, 85
Locke, John, 9, 11, 16, 114
Louis XIV, King of France, 5, 16, 23, 46
Louis XVI, King of France, 91

Mably, Gabriel Bonner de, 114
Mainz, 84, 111
Maria Theresa, Chapter II *Passim*, 64, 66, 67, 69, 74, 76, 83, 111, 120, 124–7
Martini, Karl Anton von, 10, 30, 31, 38, 39, 45, 69, 112, 114
medicine, 71–2
Mercier de la Rivière, 10
Milan, 21, 33–4, 49–51, 59, 63
Moltke, Count Hellmuth von, 86
monasteries, 8, 33–4, 59, 60, 127–9, 138–9
Montesquieu, Charles de Secondat, baron de, 9, 17, 31, 70, 99, 101, 114
Moravia, 25, 35, 46, 56, 60, 64, 73
Müller, Ignaz, 30, 34
Muratori, Lodovico, Antonio, 45, 58, 61, 71, 72

Nantes, Edict of, 64
Naples, 21, 23
natural law, 12, 13, 38, 119
Neri, Pompeo, 112
Netherlands, *see* Belgium
Newton, Sir Isaac, 3, 4
nobility, 18, 37, 47, 52–3, 63, 70, 74, 79, 87, 89, 106–10, 121, 126, 133–6, 148–50